Coaching YOU

#GIRLSONAMISSION presents:

Becoming a
Woman who Blooms

T. MCFADDIN ORDELL

Harvest Enterprises

© Theresa McFaddin Ordell

Coaching YOU
Published by #GIRLSONAMISSION Books an imprint of Harvest Enterprises
3940 Laurel Canyon Blvd., Suite 1263
Studio City, California 91604
www.girlsonamission.us

ISBN-10: 0-9667167-3-6
ISBN-13: 978-0-9667167-3-3

Cover Design: Terri McFaddin Solomon & Rick Schroeppel, Elm Street Design Studio www.elmstreetdesignstudio.net
Layout Design: Lisa Knight, www.DesignsDoneNow.com
Book Editing: Book Editing Services
Content Editing: Darryl Ordell & Stefnie Evans

SCRIPTURE QUOTES:
All rights reserved. No part of this publication may be reproduced, stored in retrieval system, or transmitted in any form or by any means – for example, electronic, photocopy, recording – without the prior written permission of the publisher. The only exception is brief quotations in printed reviews.

Because of the dynamic nature of the internet, any web addresses or links contained in this book may have changed since publication and may no longer be valid. This book is not intended to provide therapy or take the place of clinical advice or treatment from your professional counselor or mental health provider. The author takes no responsibility for any possible consequences for actions or application of information in this book to the reader.

Unless otherwise indicated, Scripture quotations are from the *Holy Bible*, New International Version (NIV) © 1973, 1978, 1984 by International Bible Society, used by permission of Zondervan Publishing House.

Other translations cited: *The Message* © 1993, 1994, 1995, 1996, 2000, 2001, 2002. Used by permission of NavPress Publishing Group. *The Amplified Bible, Old Testament* © 1965, 1987 by the Zondervan Corporation. *The Amplified New Testament* © 1958, 1987 by the Lockman Foundation. Used by permission.

Scripture quotations marked NLT are taken from the *Holy Bible*, New Living Translation, copyright 1996, 2004, 2007 by Tyndale House Foundation. Used by permission of Tyndale House Publishers, Inc., Carol Stream, Illinois 60188. All rights reserved.

The Living Bible copyright © 1971 by Tyndale House Foundation. Used by permission of Tyndale House Publishers Inc., Carol Stream, Illinois 60188. All rights reserved.

DEFINITIONS:
New Oxford American Dictionary. 2nd ed. Edited by Erin McKean. New York: Oxford University Press, 2005. Also available at http://www.oxfordamericandictionary.com/.

❧ DEDICATION ☙

In 1996 I wrote my first book and dedicated it to my mother. One of the things I wrote was that I prayed for the day I'd see a reflection of myself in my own daughter. It took fifteen years, but I now have Iris Grace Ordell.

You light up my life and bring me joy. I can coach, mentor, disciple and pastor hundreds and thousands of women, but if I don't invest in your development...all my work is for nothing. Grow, soar, flourish and bloom my gorgeous flower.

Be a divine combination of the generations before you, yet even so much more. My precious Grace-Grace, mommy loves you and knows you will impact your generation and the world for God's glory. You are born from champions, so take dominion over all the earth. You are "Perfect for God's Purpose!"

Your daddy was my first great answered prayer from the Lord, and you are no doubt my "moon". What else is in store for #teamordell? We will continue to ask God according to Isaiah 7:11.

Love, Mommy

"Ask for a sign from your GOD. Ask anything. Be extravagant. Ask for the moon."
—ISAIAH 7:11 *The Message Bible*

ACKNOWLEDGEMENTS

The love of my life, Darryl Ordell
Nothing I write makes sense until my husband revises it. He knows me. He knows how to translate me into a meaningful writer. He even rewrites some of my emails (the truth comes out). As our friend and brother, Kenny Lattimore, sings so perfectly—Darryl Ordell "remixes my old school" and tells me "I love you like...". Some of you may not understand that, but he does (and he's not here to rewrite this section). You loved me when others wouldn't, because the risk was too high for them. You are still a 2-liter in a coke can—simply explosive! I love watching you grow into a powerful man of God that does not accept compromise in God's house or our own. Love forever and for always. Took us 6 years to put out another one, but we did it!

Mommy, Terri McFaddin Solomon
Well—you told me I was taking too long to write another book, so these pages are for you. What a mentor you are! And yes, the next book is almost done. You push hard to release potential. Love that and you! In high school you gave me these words that still ring true: *The world is filled with brilliant people who will never rise above mediocrity because they aren't willing to make the sacrifice that greatness calls for.*

Hallel Chapel

To our sheep, supporters and frequent visitors, I simply love you for taking the journey with us into purpose. We conquer. We see results. We shine. We worship. We are a team and a family.

Our Spiritual Covering & Support
Bishop Gideon & Pastor Yvonne Thompson
Bishop Andrew & Pastor Viveca Merritt

#GIRLSONAMISSION & our Daughters
Zandra Palmer, Stefnie Evans, Clara Stephens, Naoe Jarmon, Amie Morehead, Marilyn Smith, Jessica Evans, Stephanie Ortiz, Alita Bailey. Natoya Evans, Ebony Tillman, Briana Jarmon, Nichole Evans, D'Crystyl Evans, Nyilah Palmer, Iris Grace Ordell, Vanessa Martinez, Safiya Bailey, Aiswariya Bailey & Jordyn Evans

Ladies, I love you so very much. You are building a gorgeous tapestry to touch women. May our girls be inspired to live for the Lord, and feel love from us that is overflowing.

To my #GIRLS & #LADIES
Roslyn Ballard, Faith Holland, Ashley Ballard, Kate Ballard, Joli Holland, Noni Daniels, Kimberly Samuels, Jenni Jones, Lillian Jones, Marlene Daniels, Mary Terry Wiley, Dolores Rivers, Dale Williams, Amber Okazaki, Domonique Rivers, Dana Rivers, April Mtyora, Mona Thompson, Tatianna Merritt, Laura Everett, Rochelle Bowman, Monique Winans, Kimberley Thompson, Jan Coleman, Keaver Brenai, Victoria Arnold, Jacqueline Plunkett, Stephanie Hazzard Smith, Jacques McNeil, Simone Green, Lynn Epps, Tige Charity, Sonya Logan, Estrelda Lewis, Alexandria Hargrove, T. Faye Griffin, Danielle Truitt, Patricia Ashley, Peggy Matthews, Juanita Scott, Starletta DuPois, Barbara Willett, Fawn Weaver, Michelle McKinney Hammond, Cheryl Sweeney, Deborah Smith Pegues, Sandra Jackson, Saundra Montgomery, Tegra Little & Janet Bailey

CONTENTS

PART 1 **QUESTIONS**

INTRODUCTION	Blooming Defined	12
CHAPTER 1	What is #GirlsOnAMission?	14
CHAPTER 2	Who are you?	20
CHAPTER 3	Who is God?	30
CHAPTER 4	Who am I?	40
CHAPTER 5	Who do you want to be?	46

PART 2 **ANSWERS**

CHAPTER 6	Types of Women	62
CHAPTER 7	Types of Goals	76
CHAPTER 8	Types of Success	92
CHAPTER 9	Types of Prayer	104
CHAPTER 10	Types of Mentoring	112

PART 3 **RESOURCES**

- COACHING ASSESSMENT QUESTIONS — 130
- YOU DEVELOPMENT QUESTIONNAIRE — 134
- DIVINE DECLARATIONS — 148
- MY TOP TEN TRUTH NUGGETS FROM SOCIAL MEDIA POSTS — 150
- WHERE TO GO FROM HERE — 154

PART ONE

QUESTIONS

༜INTRODUCTION༜
Blooming Defined

If you Ask the women at our church, Hallel Chapel, most will probably tell you, *"Pastor T. isn't the biggest fan of freshly-cut flowers"*. It's true, unfortunately. Ask my husband, and he will agree that I am not a fan; although I love receiving them. I love how they look in their temporary state of "gorgeous-ness"; however, my difficulty is that fresh-cut flowers don't stay fresh very long, because they're on their way to the big green garbage bin in the sky, an early grave. Cut flowers, no matter how pretty, are disconnected from their source of life. We can add a drop of bleach, a copper penny, flower food from the little packets, and even change the water in the vase daily, but ultimately, they've been murdered and are going to an early grave.

Have you ever received a bouquet of roses? Don't you just love the gorgeous, untainted bud of the flower? We've gotten so accustomed to seeing a half-opened rose that we don't even remember what a rose in full bloom looks like. Have you seen a bloomed rose before? All the petals are poised and opened, not afraid of the atmosphere, sun, or insects. It is quite beautiful to see a rose in full bloom, but you'll usually need to see a rose bush to see the fullness of the rose.

To bloom means to come into or be in full beauty or health. It is the state or period of greatest beauty, freshness, or vigor. To bloom is to be radiant and glowing; it is to flourish, to thrive. Just like a rose, you may have been cut and currently exist in a bud phase where you are pretty but not radiant, cute but not beautiful, rich but not wealthy.

> To bloom means to flourish, or to come into or be in full beauty or health.

This is where godly coaching is required. The Lord didn't give you breath so you could simply be a bud in a vase. He has plans to give you extraordinary life that will flourish with a radiant glow of vigor.

Now, to open up and bloom according to your planned design, you'll need to be coached from a spiritual platform. This is where the Coaching YOU book comes into …bloom…(yep, I couldn't resist) in the garden of your soul. You'll understand it better as we progress, but for now… just know the best of you is yet to be seen.

CHAPTER 1
What is #GirlsOnAMission?

I remember the first time I introduced the name of the women's group. A sister told me that it didn't really fit nor did it give the women a sense that this was something that spoke to their needs. So perhaps, you too are confused, perplexed or bewildered as to how #GIRLSONAMISSION infuses excitement into women looking for a place of spiritual encouragement. There are probably several questions.

First on the list: *Is this a ministry for young girls?* Well, actually, yes and no. It is a movement for the young girl who has been tucked away in the corridors of your mind. Some girls have been buried in memories, some forgotten by abuse, and some neglected due to generational curses. Yes, #GIRLSONAMISSION speaks to the girl inside of you who still belongs to God, but may still be battling life in pain. This little girl is the part of you that may take your woman's body and have fits of reckless sex with strangers or those that don't genuinely care. This little girl is the part of you that spends your bill money on a great pair of shoes, because she could care less about responsibility. This little girl is the part of you that eats her dessert instead of her vegetables, because she is desperately trying to soothe the inner aching and need for comfort. Second question: *Do girls from the ages of 12-19 attend our monthly Bloom Sessions?* No, we wait until they are hiding in women living in 20-something, 30-something, and 40-something bodies searching for answers. Not to say that we wouldn't do a special interaction for young girls, but ultimately, our Bloom Sessions are for grown women.

Be aware that #GIRLSONAMISSION is more than a ministry. Unfortunately, we may have overused the word, ministry, and many don't really comprehend what it means. I often wonder if people really understand ministry as it pertains to true service? Do we understand that it means our actions must be directed toward pure service that touches the heart of God? To really understand the mandate, it must be understood that #GIRLSONAMISSION is also a movement. It speaks of a forward motion to serve and support. It speaks of a group or body of girls leaving where we are to fill a void in uncharted territory. #GIRLSONAMISSION speaks to change and renewal. On our website we share the New Oxford American Dictionary definition of *mission* as "*a strongly felt aim or ambition or calling.*" It actually originated from the Latin word denoting the sending of the Holy Spirit into the world. So when we speak of fulfilling our mission, we are instruments being sent out by the Holy Spirit into a world in need of service, and we go together as a unit and team of women. So ultimately, #GIRLSONAMISSION is a ministry movement of women coming to God as daughters, "his girls", pliable, submitted, and open to discovery asking him to use us as individuals and a collective force to meet needs.

Recently, I took my little girl to an amusement park. Well, actually I take her there often, because we have a family pass. Walking in the park gate, I'm always mesmerized by the preteen girls running free from ride to ride with their friends. They smile, talk, scream, and laugh without apology, as they enjoy every little tiny moment of pleasure. They tackle frightening roller coasters but still get on the rides for small children. Girls enjoy, exist, and embrace. Girls are free.

One night, I ventured off from my husband and daughter and rode a roller coaster alone. The girl in me challenged the woman I've become to just take the dips and turns with complete abandonment. I fought the feeling to look like I was off to a meeting. I was alone and struggled to just enjoy the thrill of the unknown while the wind twirled around my face. Surprisingly, it was a fight to just let the girl in me scream, throw my hands up in the air and be in the moment. Women so often have to be "in control" We have to be aware of our surroundings. But girls know they have someone else, like a parent or guardian, on duty taking care of the heavy lifting and being their eyes.

My primary roles in life are being a mom, wife, pastor, and mentor. So I am constantly caring for others. My husband, however, has been urging me to get a "thing"...something that feeds my inner girl. When I worked as a COO or a non-profit, I didn't make a glamorous salary, but I still afforded myself a membership to a wonderful spa, Burke Williams. It was my unwinding zone and my relaxation space. Never-

> **#GirlsOnAMission is for the young girl in every woman. Think of it as tapping into the heart of a seasoned woman while releasing the courage of a young girl.**

theless, as a woman, I had to reexamine our monthly budget when I stepped down from this position to assist in the running of our church. It was time to be wise and practical, but somewhere in this decision I imprisoned my inner girl, telling her there wasn't enough money for her to exist. Yes, irritation and frustration were a direct result of not having an outlet. My mind said it was too costly to have a thing. So I budgeted for my husband's thing and worked hard to give my daughter her thing, but Mommy was too busy being an adult woman.

Until, I found myself in my daughter's world. She's a little girl, and the amusement park pass speaks to that freedom. I was the woman taking her, and my inner little girl started to beg for a chance to play too. So, after several trips, I finally realized that the amusement park should also become my thing So it's now my therapy between juggling family, pastoring, coaching, and mentoring. In addition, I do a lot of walking, so my body wins, too. I don't just take her on the rides restraining my own abandonment, but now "we" go on the rides together. There's something freeing when you twirl, swing, or brave a dip while letting out a scream or a laugh.

As a result of needing a thing while I complete my mission, my desire is to coach women to find their mission, but it only works if they find balance by letting their inner girl out to play and explore. So I work #GIRLSONAMISSION to include monthly meetings outdoors, or working with arts and crafts, while teaching biblical principles. I deliberately have my weekly update sessions with my ladies in cute coffee houses. When planning large meetings, I make efforts to build on a fun theme so that the little girls in the ladies always feel like there's a safe platform to speak and work through their own journey of release and freedom.

So I said all this to say, Yes...#GIRLSONAMISSION is for the young girl in every woman. Think of it as tapping into the heart of a seasoned woman while releasing the courage of a young girl. So, let the pretty little God's girl inside of you have her thing; it will make Coaching YOU so much more relevant.

Enjoy!

COACHING QUESTIONS

What was your favorite thing to do as a young girl?

What do you and your "girl" friends do for fun besides going out to eat?

Do you have any young girls whom you spend time with in your life?

COACHING VERSE

[MARK 5:41]
He took her by the hand and said to her, "*Talitha koum!*"
(Which means, "little girl, I say to you, get up!")

DIVINE DECLARATION

Lord, I will find my "thing." Help me keep in touch with my inner little girl so that I will be pliable, submitted, and open to discovery.

CHAPTER 2
Who are you?

This question may seem basic. Some would answer with one-word nouns: wife, sister, mother, friend, single, nurse, athlete, attorney, etc. Others would answer with phrases: I'm a daughter of a King, I'm a rape victim, I'm a recovering addict, I'm an unmarried woman, I'm loved. But ultimately, some may simply say, "I don't really know." Then the question becomes, Is it okay not to really know who you are? This is one of the most abstract questions we'll ever get asked. Is it actually a philosophical question? Or could it have answers based on our age, place in life, socioeconomic status, or race?

Perhaps if you want to know who you are, then you may consider what you've accomplished. You may say: I am a state champion track star; I am a cancer overcomer. I am a college graduate. The only downfall with basing our existence on what we've achieved is that we forget that we are constantly evolving and moving forward. So, should we then base our answer on where we want to be in life, or what we dream of becoming, or what our education states we are being trained to accomplish? All in all, this could become a frustrated journey that can take us on a rollercoaster ride of highs and lows as we consider our failures and our successes.

Perhaps the best part of this question can also be found in mixing it all up! Yes, are you just a woman, or are you just middle class? Are you only a graduate or a nurse? Let's try another technique. How about we throw the words in the air and see if we can find answers in the shake-up. Ready? Toss! Here's what we now have: "Who you are." Or even "You are who…" Remember the best answer for a product's potential in development is never found by simply examining the product parts, but in an in depth conversation with the Creator of the product. The Creator is the designer and knows the original intent. The Creator knows the ingredients. The Creator knows the investment. The Creator knows the potential. So if you are ever asked, "Who are you?" you must actually learn to point to the designer's insight and declare what you were told when you went on your own personal discovery of self with the ultimate designer.

If you know the one who made you, then you will find that he will speak to you from the standpoint of knowing who you are. He will speak to you from the standpoint of "you are who I created in secret." To understand yourself, you must go to the owner's manual, the Bible, subsection Psalms, chapter 139.

> For you created my inmost being;
> you knit me together in my mother's womb.
> I praise you because I am fearfully
> and wonderfully made;
> your works are wonderful, I know that full well.
> My frame was not hidden from you
> when I was made in the secret place,
> when I was woven together in the depths of the earth.
> Your eyes saw my unformed body;
> all the days ordained for me were written in your book

> before one of them came to be.
> How precious to me are your thoughts, God!
> How vast is the sum of them!
>
> —PSALM 139:13-17

> You keep track of all my sorrows.
> You have collected all my tears in your bottle.
> You have recorded each one in your book.
>
> —PSALM 56:8 *New Living Translation*

This Bible chapter creates a setting of a divine inventor alone in a lab with every possible resource. His lab holds a vault of personalities, an endless treasure chest of skill and gifting, a walk-in closet of thought patterns and physical wrapping paper. There are design plans, a vast book of days, and even tears. Yes, every moment of

$$\frac{[\text{THE EQUATION}]}{+ \text{You}} = \text{Wonderfully Made}$$

your life, and every tear of joy and sorrow. All defining who you are. All pointing to "you are who I created in secret." So honestly, you may not be able to fully answer the question of, "Who are you?" But as you sit with the Master Creator, you listen as he declares who you are. And as you listen without complaint, regret or doubt, you reply simply by repeating Psalm 139:14, "I praise you." Yes, then you begin to understand the relationship of the equation: I + YOU. "I, the creature, will praise You, the Creator, because I have finally discovered that whoever I am, I am wonderfully made." This was no assembly line rush job filling an order of Hispanic men in Mexico, or African-American women in Harlem, or French women in Europe. It was a secret creation to be displayed upon completion. Everything was so important that the Creator wrote a book recording every second, and He holds your every tear.

The following becomes true when reading Psalm 139:

- You can never escape his presence
- You were made in secret
- You were woven together in the depths of the earth
- You are fearfully and wonderfully made
- When you awake, he is still with you
- He has searched you
- He knows when you sit and rise
- He knows every word before it's spoken
- He created your inmost being
- His eyes saw your unformed body
- Even the darkness is not dark to him

So, with all of these facts, I praise You. My identity is found in my Creator, not in me, the creature. When I was single, I bought a BMW X5. Wow, did I love that SUV! Whew, it had all types of buttons, sensors, and gadgets. It was a machine of power. I enjoyed every ride I took, whether to the store around the corner or on the road driving across country. Because of the spectacular design, not once did I take my BMW to a Ford dealer. Not once did I take my BMW to a Mercedes dealer. For every need, every problem or question, I went to a certified BMW dealer to gain the expertise of the Creator. Not one time during the course of ownership was I turned away because they did not know the details about my BMW X5 I had purchased. Eventually, when I married, we bought a Honda Odyssey (big shift, right?). While signing the contract, there was a clause that stated that when repairs were needed, we would agree that we'd first take our Honda to a certified Honda dealer, and not a third-party vendor to fix whatever was wrong. Yes, we agreed to these terms, because they knew the car they'd created.

Now, since God created you, he knows who you are. Once you go to the Source, then you begin to walk in the destiny found in the pages of the book he wrote about you. You even find power knowing that your tears are collected, held, and understood. The creature loves the Creator because identity begins to unfold. Once identity is uncovered, then direction is revealed. A rhythm is found in life. As long as there's a connection to the Source, every resource is provided. And finally, you can begin to formulate an answer to the question: "Who are you?" because you are being told constantly who you are.

But one day, you become comfortable in your knowledge of who you are and neglect to visit the Source of it all, because there seems to be more than enough resources and tasks to accomplish. One day, you think you know everything for uncovering your direction. You forget that a daily discovery keeps you focused for new updates and Creator downloads. You assume you don't have to walk with God in the cool of the day every day having conversations of discovery. And it happens one day that the Creator comes to the creature and presents questions to you about your disappearance and conversations with others about who you are. He wants answers from his creation.

> And they heard the sound of the LORD God walking in the garden in the cool of the day, and Adam and his wife hid themselves from the presence of the LORD God among the trees of the garden. Then the LORD God called to Adam and said to him, "Where are you?"
> —GENESIS 3:8-9

> You were running the race so well.
> Who has held you back from following the truth?
> —GALATIANS 5:7 *New Living Translation*

See, when you begin to disconnect from the Creator, you awaken only to find that you've wandered away from the power of Psalm 139. You find that you've forgotten some basic truths. You've forgotten your power statement: "I praise you." You begin to bargain. You begin to explain. You begin to search; but the Creator never moved. In fact, he is always at his post; but where are you? When you present yourself for questioning, Your Creator begins to remind you of your past struggles that you overcame and the work it took for you to refocus on your true identity. Here's the process he takes you through.

> On the day you were born your cord was not cut, nor were you washed with water to make you clean, nor were you rubbed with salt or wrapped in cloths. No one looked on you with pity or had compassion

> *enough to do any of these things for you.*
> *Rather, you were thrown out into the open field,*
> *for on the day you were born you were despised.*
> *Then I passed by and saw you kicking about*
> *in your blood, and as you lay there*
> *in your blood I said to you, "Live!"*
>
> —EZEKIEL 16:4-6

Yes, this is why the Creator can look at you and declare who you are, because He not only created you but he also rescued you and spoke a word of power over you when He simply said: **"LIVE!"** So the equation must now be reassessed: **I + YOU + WHO.** God wants to know the "who" responsible for why you may have wandered from fulfilling the divine plan over your life. *"Who has held you back?"* You may not be in proper proximity to the Lord, but you can still hear these questions.

Now consider this question: "How can you recover?" This book is all about asking questions through a process called coaching. Yes, many of us seek a mentor, life coach, facilitator, or discipleship leader, all in order to "recover." The following definition of coaching will give you an idea of why you are finding extensive questioning in this book. Let's examine this process:

[THE NEW EQUATION]

$$\frac{\begin{array}{r}I\\+\ You\\+\ Who\end{array}}{=\text{Recovery Needed}}$$

> **COACHING** *is training or development in which a person called a "coach" supports a learner in achieving a specific personal or professional goal. Occasionally, "coaching" may mean an informal relationship between two people, of whom one has more experience and expertise than the other and offers advice and guidance as the latter learns; but coaching differs from mentoring in focusing on the specifics of doing something successfully, as opposed to general overall development. Some coaches use a style in which they ask questions and offer opportunities to challenge the learner to find his or her own answers. This helps the learner find answers and new ways of perceiving and performing in the society; based on their own values, preferences and perspectives.*
>
> Renton, Jane (2009). *Coaching and Mentoring: What They Are and How to Make the Most of Them.* New York: Bloomberg Press.

Now, in my approach to coaching you, I am looking to support you in achieving the goal of getting clear on your life's mission from the Lord, as my focus is your spiritual development. This coaching as you read will be accomplished by asking questions, developing your searching skills in the word of God, and prepping you for deeper mentoring. Coaching is the first step to me handing you the tools you need to reconnect with your Creator. It doesn't necessarily require several phone calls, homework submission, or studying with me on a consistent basis as in discipleship training. Coaching is reminding you of your power in God, tossing you the ball, giving you tips on how to score and cheering as you make touch downs or 3 pointers. So, are you ready to discover who you are? Great— let's get to work!

COACHING QUESTIONS

Who are you?

Where are you in your current state of living? Aimless? Direction-focused? Beginning to bloom? Explain.

Who has held you back and kept you from developing?

COACHING VERSE

[PSALM 139:23-24]
Search me, O God, and know my heart; test me and know my anxious thoughts. Point out anything in me that offends you, and lead me along the path of everlasting life.

DIVINE DECLARATION

I, the creature will praise you, the Creator, because I'm pretty wonder-full! Lord, I want to know who I am full well, free of doubt, and accepting of what you decide to change.

CHAPTER 3
Who is God?

Yes, I am fully aware of how crazy this question sounds. Yes, I am fully aware that I'd have to write an entire book to just scratch the surface of who He is. Yes, I am fully aware that a book has actually already been written, the Bible, and it took several powerful, God-ordained authors to compile this holy, consecrated and God-breathed life manual. When I ask, "Who is God?" I'm speaking in regards to Coaching YOU. If he is your Creator, if all roads lead to what he has required of you, then it is only necessary to know who he is as you prepare to bloom as the creature he intended.

In this context, we will examine only three facets of his character and identity. This is in no way meant to limit his omniscience or omnipotence. This is just the beginning of coaching you on your journey of spiritual development. I believe if you see the Master of the Universe and God of the Angel Armies in these three distinctions, then you will not only see the power he commands, but also the power he extends to you.

Before I unveil these three positions of power, let me clearly state that the God I speak of came to earth in the person of Jesus Christ. The force of your coaching platform must be clearly understood from a monotheistic teaching, that Jesus is the only God, and not a polytheistic worldview, that various religions can bring about spiritual development. As unpopular as this sounds, I cannot in good faith train or coach you while supporting syncretism (combining of different religions, cultures, or schools of thought) as a way for you to bloom into being the woman the Lord created you to be. I train from the platform that Christ was God in flesh and died on the cross to free you and me from sin and shame. You must understand the five basic steps defining Jesus as Lord in the fabric of the Christian faith: the birth, life, death, resurrection and second coming of Christ. Without these basic truths, there is no growth. Who is God? For the Christian, Jesus is God, the Messiah, and our Savior.

Now, let us go on to explore these three steps of power in understanding who God is. First step, he is the **God of Peace.** This title doesn't state that he has access to peace, but that he is actually the Author and Giver of peace (Hebrews 13:20 Amplified). Consider these scriptural platforms:

> And may the God of peace Himself sanctify you through and through [separate you from profane things, make you pure and wholly consecrated to God]; and may your spirit and soul and body be preserved sound and complete [and found] blameless at the coming of our Lord Jesus Christ (the Messiah).
>
> —1 THESSALONIANS 5:23 *The Amplified Version*

> The God of peace will soon crush Satan under your feet. The grace of our Lord Jesus be with you.
>
> —ROMANS 16:20

The word of God is the power of spiritual coaching! If I stop typing and sell you a book with these two verse and 100 blank pages, you can soar and become a magnificent creature! One of the best parts about the Lord being the God of Peace is that we must redefine what peace actually is. We often think of it as just calm, tranquil or

> *Once you have been cut away from a drama-filled lifestyle, then you have a better chance to preserve your spirit, soul, and body.*

soft; however, we now see the power delivered when we see peace in its full capacity. In order for peace to silence the disorderly things all around it, there must be a solid base of power in operation where the God of Peace sanctifies, preserves, and crushes. Peace has to truly be maintained by the almighty Creator.

Having a life of peace is more powerful than having great wealth. Wealth, fame, or money does not guarantee that you have control over your environment. When you understand that he is the God of Peace that separates you from profane things and makes you pure, you then understand that he offers you the precious gift of ruling over your surroundings with this base of power. When you have a life that stands outside of shame and condemnation, you can finally see how to overpower insanity because you walk with the God that speaks to storms in your life. It doesn't mean that you are no longer subjected to pain and situations of discomfort, but once you have been cut away from a drama-filled lifestyle, then you have a better chance to preserve your spirit, soul, and body.

The great Christian writer, Watchman Nee, taught us that our spirit is the part of us that communes with the Lord, while the body communes with the world. The soul is the prize, being pulled either way because it houses our thoughts, emotions, and our actions. How do we know whether or not the Lord or the world will take possession of our soul? Whoever gets fed the most will prevail. If everything we do feeds into the chaotic existence of society and carnality, then we wander away from the sanctifying work of the God of Peace. This results in a loss of control, because Satan cannot be crushed under our feet. In order to take authority over drama, we must remain close by and consecrated to the God of Peace. He said that this crushing would take place "soon"; therefore, we must be ready at any given time to exercise our authority that comes when our spirit, soul, and body are found blameless. All of this power is delivered into our hands when we answer the question, "who is God?" with the bold answer, "he is the God of Peace." The most powerful component of this verse, passage, declaration is that to ensure that the crushing takes place, he sends the most favorable companion, his grace. Grace is God's undeserved kindness. Romans 16:20 doesn't just say that we'll crush Satan, but

Whoever gets fed the most will prevail.

that we'll do this because as we wait for the "soon," grace will be present in our lives to ensure victory in areas where we may make mistakes along the journey.

Secondly, he is the **God of Hope.** He makes the unthinkable, possible. He is the Source of hope. He is the well from which we draw.

Hope can be frightening if the God of Peace has not already been working in our lives to sanctify us from fear and doubt. Hope demands that we expect, that we keep looking out the window and that we remain steadfast in a lifestyle of faith. Hope makes you look crazy, because you refuse to give up.

And here comes the entrance of peace again, but this time it is accompanied by joy. I like to think of joy as smiling at the invisible blessing promised by God, even if others can't see that it is coming your way. There may not be any circumstances to drive you to have joy, but you possess it as a result of trusting in the God of Hope. Imagine you are an empty container longing to hold a liquid. You were created to contain. You sit empty, just wanting to be used. This wanting is made of a substance called hope. Finally, the Master comes and begins to pour into you... this empty container. There are two ingredients that he combines, joy and peace. It is fine, but you wonder if you could have contained something else, something greater but you don't question, you opt to trust. You remain still as the liquid gets closer to your brim, and then suddenly you feel the mixture gushing over the top and flowing out of you onto anything that was close to you. Now the strangest thing has occurred—the mixture of joy and peace has evolved into a new product called hope.

How did this happen? The power of the Holy Spirit began to stir things up on the inside, and now the God of Hope produced hope inside of you as a result of you submitting to this metamorphosis. How does the power of the Holy Spirit operate in your life? Great question. Because he is the Spirit of Truth, it can take place in three ways: *comfort, counsel, and conviction* (John 14:26 AMP; 16:7-8 NIV). His comfort holds you while you wait in hope. His counsel instructs you on how the hope will materialize in your life. His conviction maintains proper order, with your hope keeping it God-driven not fantasy-driven.

Lastly, when we think of how to answer "who is God?" in the equation of coaching you into blooming, we must acknowledge that **God is Love.** Sis, you just can't exclude love from your development. Through every disappointment, through every hurt and every setback, love pushes you through to healing. This is what separates a woman who looks to bloom and joins other #GIRLSONAMISSION from one who looks to promote her agenda and live in an ivory tower, alone.

> Dear friends, let us continue to love one another, for love comes from God. Anyone who loves is a child of God and knows God. But anyone who does not love does not know God, for God is love.
>
> —1 JOHN 4:7-8 *New Living Translation*

> And so we know and rely on the love God has for us. God is love. Whoever lives in love lives in God, and God in them.
>
> —1 JOHN 4:16

Probably one of the greatest attacks on women is the theft of love. It appears that Satan attempts to deceive women into thinking that every act of abuse, deception, or assault means that God did not love them. And so hate and bitterness anchor in her soul as she builds a fake wall of protection that only leads to isolation. We need each other. Where was the God of Peace, the God of Hope and the God of Love when you were violated? He was focused on the blooming process. Yes, in order for you to grow, some ingredients were required in your life. I teach that there are five ingredients God uses to cultivate you to become larger and greater over time.

INGREDIENTS FOR GROWTH

Crap
All things work together, even the disgusting events,
to go back and create life.

Dirt
You have to feel the pileup of life around your roots
so you have something to attach to. It's not pretty, but necessary.

Water
Mixes with dirt and becomes mud;
avoid feeling stuck—it cleanses you.

Sun
The rays from heaven renew, revive, and restore.

Pruning
After you begin to grow, some stuff has to be trimmed or cut off
as you go through life so that you can flourish even more.

When Satan attempted to knock out your ability to love, he thought he could uproot you. He didn't realize that his efforts only transplanted you into the Lord's own garden and strategically put you under God's personal care. It's not too late for you to produce fruit. The key is that you have to love. And in order to love, you have to live in God, and God has to live in you and then love through you. Yes, it's probably true, there are some people you cannot fathom loving. BUT, if God lives in you, he will do the work while you become the instrument. It's amazing what a transplant can do! So let's get into a new zone of living. Look at all you've been through and relocate the hurt. Relocate your love. Get back to God and allow the sanctification process to begin by allowing the God of Peace into your heart. Get back to God and allow him to fill your container with joy and peace and let it morph into hope, because the God of Hope is working with the Holy Spirit by his side. Get back to God and allow him to be love in you and through you. I am confident you will find yourself when you answer the question, "Who is God?"

> But the godly shall flourish like palm trees and
> grow tall as the cedars of Lebanon.
> For they are transplanted into the Lord's own garden
> and are under his personal care.
> Even in old age they will still produce fruit
> and be vital and green.
> —PSALM 92:12-14

CHAPTER QUESTIONS

Which one of these three components of God do you need the most based upon your life history? Explain?

Are you religious but not anchored in who God is?

Have you opened yourself up to syncretism?

COACHING VERSE

[1 JOHN 3:1-3]

See what great love the Father has lavished on us, that we should be called children of God! And that is what we are! The reason the world does not know us is that it did not know him. Dear friends, now we are children of God, and what we will be has not yet been made known. But we know that when Christ appears,[a] we shall be like him, for we shall see him as he is. All who have this hope in him purify themselves, just as he is pure.

DIVINE DECLARATION

God of the Angel Armies comes to my rescue with unlimited resources of hope, peace, and love. He's the Almighty! I have been transplanted into the Lord's own garden!

CHAPTER 4
Who am I?

Quite frankly, according to social media I am a nobody. I have less than 500 Twitter followers, and not quite 2,000 Facebook friends. For about a year, I've pastored a church alongside my husband that has yet to gain a solid 50 members. Yes, with those qualifications, in a social media-driven world, I would not appear to be the coach you'd look for.

But God says I have lived a life of tragedy turned into triumph. Born with three fingers on each hand and orthopedic discrepancies with the length of my legs, I've fought for my survival. Who am I? I know who I am not. I am not insecure. Considering my history of being raised by a single mother after my father died when I was three, I could be a mental basket case. But no, I remain extremely confident in Christ. My body is just a package, but my inner woman is quite powerful, despite limited popularity. I have battle scars. I am a woman who stayed single until I was 41 years old because I refused to marry a man who didn't love me. I am a mother who birthed a miracle daughter from a dilapidated womb at 42 years old, and who is still asking God if I may be blessed to birth a son as I knock on 47 years of age. I am a fighter.

Some of the most extraordinary women I know are not famous. My greatest fear for this generation is that people only respect fame and money, not endurance and stability. Over the years, many have coached, mentored and discipled me. There's a wealth of deposits that have been made; therefore, I walk in a solid anointing with much to give away to other women. None of this is stated in arrogance, and my most notable successes in ministry have been in mentoring and discipling women to do more. My encounters with rejection, fear, and failure have equipped me to survive. My beauty is hidden underneath the skin, so it makes me glow with a supernatural attraction. Because I am certain of my identity, I can rearrange the chapter question and ask you… "am I who" is to coach you?

When I invest in a person's life, the commitment is real. It's a disservice to you to go easy on yourself when you desire to change. Wasting time is for fake people building social media rankings. I was trained to show you how to dig deep. This means you are responsible for your own homework. As a result of all of this truth, a lot of "girls" have walked away from my discipleship process calling me crazy and many other things I've chosen to forget. This interaction is not about me, so if someone chooses to step away from mentoring or discipleship, then perhaps the real truth is that they just can't look in the mirror. You have to realize **Discipleship is not for wimps.** Later in the book, we'll review step 2 of the You Spiritual Development Model with more detail. But here is a breakdown of the four methods used to build your spiritual development:

INTERACTION	Coaching	Mentoring	Discipling	Pastoring
PROXIMITY	Insight from afar	Closer interaction and access	Up close and personal	Doing life together
PROGRAM	ANNUAL: A Date With God	MONTHLY: Bloom Sessions	WEEKLY: Me Management Classes	Constant shepharding

This chart is a detailed list of how I pour into the lives of others. And once I turned 40, I stopped "wasting my oil". When it becomes clear that someone doesn't want a deposit from me, I stop pouring. People who really want it, reach for you regardless of fear, uncertainty, or a lack of understanding. They let nothing stand in their way of receiving what God has for them. Don't be surprised if your coach, mentor, or discipler is unorthodox or has random requirements. It builds trust and shows if you are willing to go through and respect the process. A lot of women have pledged a sorority. To get into the club, the journey is rough before they cross over into sisterhood. As bizarre as it may seem, none of these ladies thinks it is weird. Consequently, when you desire to grow in God, you cannot look at mentoring or discipleship requirements different from pledging. This is not to hurt you, but simply to grow you!

Want to really throw mentoring out of whack? Try telling someone how to coach or mentor you. If they are serious and qualified, they won't stand for you trying to instruct them. Expect a coach or mentor to be confident. If they are insecure, please run for your life. If you can manipulate them, they are not for you. If you run the show, then you are both creating a dysfunctional relationship. If there is no submission to his or her authority, there can be no change or display of power in your life. A real coach or mentor should intimidate you or keep you guessing. There should be things required of you that you don't understand. And finally, a coach or mentor should have battle scars and total humility in their submission to Christ.

All in all, you have to decide how much of your mentor you can take. Because with every victory, they can point out where growth is needed. Most mentors have had failures. They should also have boundaries. Don't use their shortcomings as an excuse for you to quit. Their mistakes create a teaching platform for them to help guide you to your future. Likewise their boundaries set the stage for understanding discipline. There are things in my life that I value dearly and need for existence. For these things I will always put coaching, mentoring, and discipleship last: my marriage, my child, and my extended family. Perhaps this will keep me from being famous, but those three things are my lifeline to reality and keep me sharp for God's use. When I see women sacrifice their family on the altar of career or fame, I am baffled. My husband and I call our daughter, our dog and ourselves #teamordell. Second only to walking with the Lord is being with them. We roll deep. We are often together 80-90 percent of the time. We're wired this way. We get off track when we're not doing life side-by-side. That's not everyone's calling, but this is how #teamordell gets down. As a result, I often have to disconnect from those who want to take me without taking the whole team. When you get me, you'll experience Pastor Darryl and Iris Grace. This is a fact. So, I then must be willing to be transparent. You have the opportunity to see my marriage and my parenting. You get to see me soar and at times crash and live in the realm of grace and mercy on a daily basis.

I did ministry for 20 years before getting married. I decided my schedule. My traveling only affected my then dogs/girls, Peace and Joy. And now I sit, trying to figure out how to share the load, write a book while raising a 4-year-old, and grow a relevant church in an era when church is not so popular. Oh, and still find time for date night! This is where my survival, fighting, and achieving skills become real. This is where Theresa is exposed. Yes, the lady who is called to help people but has difficulty remembering names. Yes, the lady who was once the little girl who had to endure finger pointing from those who didn't understand her handicaps. Yes, the lady who is trying to figure out how to combat her hair thinning when she desires to be authentic.

So, I say all that to say, "am I who" the Lord will use to help you bloom through coaching, mentoring, discipling or maybe pastoring? I guess we'll find out.

COACHING QUESTIONS

Can you submit to a person who isn't prominent? Why or why not?

Do you want a coach, a mentor, or a discipler? Explain your need.

Do you run when growth becomes uncomfortable and revealing?

BONUS QUESTION: As you look in the mirror of your life, do you like what you see? Explain your answer.

COACHING VERSE

[2 TIMOTHY 4:9-15 *New Living Translation*]
Timothy, please come as soon as you can. Demas has deserted me because he loves the things of this life and has gone to Thessalonica. Crescens has gone to Galatia, and Titus has gone to Dalmatia. Only Luke is with me. Bring Mark with you when you come, for he will be helpful to me in my ministry. I sent Tychicus to Ephesus. When you come, be sure to bring the coat I left with Carpus at Troas. Also bring

my books, and especially my papers.[a] Alexander the coppersmith did me much harm, but the Lord will judge him for what he has done. Be careful of him, for he fought against everything we said.

DIVINE DECLARATION

God I will allow you to use my mentor to fashion me to be the best I can be, by teaching me through their victories and challenges. I will respect the process.

CHAPTER 5
Who do you want to be?

Ultimately, who do you want to be? How do you want to evolve and bloom? Blooming occurs in stages, so as you take growth steps, "do you know where you're going to?" (Cue theme song from the movie *Mahogany*.) This may not be an easy question. I dare say that coaching will ever present easy questions. It should cause you to think, study and probe yourself and consider your metamorphosis. Many women are just living life day to day on a mediocre level not even considering who they want to be in reality. Some of you will say that you know the answer already, and you are waving your hand furiously in the air trying to get the coach's attention— *"Oh oo ooo, I know! I want to be a rich woman with lots of clothes and shoes!"* Another says, *"I want to be a powerful corporate giant giving orders and making deals!"* And yet another says, *"Pick me, pick me! I want to be famous and married to a wealthy businessman and fly around the world doing photo shoots!"* Okay, okay … everyone put your hand down. That all speaks to temporal things, perception, and minimal comfort until one of those things is lost—the money, the business, or the man. Let's dig deeper. How about I offer three suggestions and you can choose either one, or all of the above. This way, if you do happen to become rich, famous, or powerful… you'll have some staying power! Deal?

The question, who do you want to be, can be reduced to one word—**IDENTITY.** This is a word that is associated with particular groupings as people seek to explain themselves. However, it is defined as the fact of being who you are. It is distinctiveness, uniqueness, or differentness. I like the word "differentness" because most of us work hard to find "sameness." We want to fit in and not stand out. When we see someone standing outside of the group, we may envy their freedom from insecurity. Accepting your identity of differentness in God means you are not ashamed, and you are willing to be unique in the call he has for you. You are comfortable being who God has declared you to be. This is a matter with a spiritual foundation. For example, I am comfortable having three fingers, because I understand the power I possess to walk in freedom while showing my hands, because I am wonderfully made. I am also comfortable walking in my anointing as a pastor, even though those who don't believe women can walk in this call do not often receive it in a positive light. You have to know your identity, respect your spiritual power and ignore those who don't get it.

Let's rehearse this scripture another time. It is truly a platform for the book and explains the power God has to redefine who you are:

And may the God of peace Himself sanctify you through and through [separate you from profane things, make you pure and wholly consecrated to God]; and may your spirit and soul and body be preserved sound and complete [and found] blameless at the coming of our Lord Jesus Christ (the Messiah).

—1 THESSALONIANS 5:23 *The Amplified Bible*

I just can't get enough of this power-packed word from God. It is a powerful prayer for understanding identity. Three critical words are used in the Amplified version: **sanctify, separate, and consecrate.** The visual of this spiritual surgical procedure is God seeing you as priceless, so he cuts you away from profane things seeking to identify you. This process alone often takes time. It's the tale of the eagle raised as a chicken and fighting the Creator, because he wants to continue walking around pecking the ground and never dreams of soaring through the air with expanded wings. To be sanctified makes you legitimate and acceptable in the Lord's eyes. It's a spiritual Cinderella story. You are a holy daughter of the King, valuable, without flaw. Profane living chips away at your identity. So God uses separation and rejection to pull you into your true self. This often involves detoxing you from average people, below average activities and unnatural activities. He longs to consecrate you, meaning he declares you as sacred and valuable. Profane is foul, vulgar, and filthy. So even if you have done things of this nature, the creature was not created this way. Remember that God, the Creator, has plans to make you pure, which is not diluted by the wrong people, places or activities. So in Psalm 139, he explores the depths he'll go to, to sanctify you because he knows you:

> You know everything I'm going to say
> before I start the first sentence.
> I look behind me and you're there,
> then up ahead and you're there, too—
> your reassuring presence, coming and going.
> This is too much, too wonderful—
> I can't take it all in!

Is there any place I can go to avoid your Spirit?
to be out of your sight?
If I climb to the sky, you're there!
If I go underground, you're there!
If I flew on morning's wings
to the far western horizon,
You'd find me in a minute—
you're already there waiting!
Then I said to myself, "Oh, he even sees me in the dark!
At night I'm immersed in the light!"
It's a fact: darkness isn't dark to you;
night and day, darkness and light,
they're all the same to you.
Oh yes, you shaped me first inside, then out;
you formed me in my mother's womb.
I thank you, High God—you're breathtaking!
Body and soul, I am marvelously made!
I worship in adoration—what a creation!
You know me inside and out,
you know every bone in my body;
You know exactly how I was made, bit by bit,
how I was sculpted from nothing into something.

—PSALM 139:5-16 *The Message Bible*

The "old folks" used to say that to be a consecrated and sanctified girl meant you didn't wear lipstick or pants or go to the movies. Oddly enough, there's some truth there if you go deeper. At the end of the day, being holy or sanctified means you have been surgically removed from profane living and now you are pure and preserved as blameless in your spirit, your soul, and even your body. You have been retrained as the eagle you are; you can soar above being common. You are a princess that doesn't mingle in average living. The process of being separated didn't establish a pride-driven mentality, because you had to come to grips with your identity, so you have humbly made that transition by rehearsing on a daily basis who you are. You now relate to the Lord differently because the Creator is constantly molding you and reminding you of your worth.

LET'S REVIEW YOUR OPTIONS FOR THE NEW YOU:

Whoever you become, you must not leave the girl in you behind as you develop. Remember her? If you lock her up, she throws a tantrum, because she needs to find identity, too. So in your becoming, find the balance with your girl and your woman. The options will help you understand better.

> [OPTION #1]
> A girl defended
> + a woman restored
> ―――――――――――
> = My Future Self

I often teach that salvation is not a one-time occurrence. Salvation happens in four different ways: your initial contact with Christ; your personal confirmation; your moment of need; and your responsibility. So it's a process, and scripture teaches that we are "being" saved. Every little girl deserves a defender to protect her, teach her, and shape her. Many of us feel as though we grew up unsheltered, unprotected, or disregarded; and therefore, we were left as open prey in a depraved world. Did God abandon us as little girls? As one who survived my own share of being open prey, I must say that his defense of us is often intertwined with his growing us. It means that there will be tears, but it also means that he collects those tears as a reminder of how much our victory cost and how much he loves us. I love how the prophet Isaiah starts the following passage, "In that day you will say..." It is as though God is saying, the day you find out who you are and wake up to my ultimate plan, you will respond in this manner.

> In that day you will say:
> "I will praise you, LORD.
> Although you were angry with me,
> your anger has turned away
> and you have comforted me.
> Surely God is my salvation;
> I will trust and not be afraid.
> The LORD, the LORD himself,
> is my strength and my defense;
> he has become my salvation."
> With joy you will draw water
> from the wells of salvation.
> —ISAIAH 12:1-3

God is saying that when Jesus is born into your heart, you will discover your identity, and you will say, even though being open prey felt like God's anger, I am now seeing his plan over my life. He comforts me, saves me, defends me...and I am drinking in total and complete joy! When the girl in you sees the woman you have become restored – *WHEWWWW!* It is as though you are outside of time, and he heals and plays catch-up with your past and future in your present, all at the same time! Remember that mission you're called to complete? Well, the beginning of it is usually birthed out of your pain and suffering.

When my daughter was an infant, I held her one night and just began to cry over her future hurt. I'm not saying I was planning to turn her over to intense life pain, but I ultimately knew she was born and given to me in order to complete a mission. This is why I do my part to create a childhood for her, because God allows life to cut us. I want to mix in joy with the coming tears. But thank God for his restoration that ties the cutting and the consecration altogether. I weep over what may happen in her life, but I rejoice in advance at how it will be used to make her a lifetime member of #GIRLSONAMISSION when she steps into womanhood. To be restored is to be brought back to the former condition. It speaks of being brought back and repaired as the Creator intended, before the tears. So no matter what you've had to go through, God knows that he alone is able to restore you to a girl shaped in innocence. Do you want to be a girl defended and a woman restored? That may be better than being famous.

[OPTION #2]
A girl loved
+ a woman confident
___
= My Future Self

I know that there is no better intangible substance on the planet than pure and perfect LOVE! I believe this is why the Bible doesn't say he is the God of Love, but that God IS love. The fabric and substance of our deepest longing is love. It is God. Show me an unloved little girl, and I'll show you a hateful, insecure woman longing to gain the love she missed. A lack of love and a fullness of insecurity can cause a woman to appear ugly, old, and used. Honestly, even with gorgeous features, rich hair, and flawless skin, her ugliness rises and presses its way to the surface of her heart and oozes out in pictures, conversation, and her overall presentation.

When you grow up unloved, you fight and claw every day you live. You're angry. You're hurt, so you hurt others. You are a mean boss, a conniving friend, and a manipulative wife, all because you want someone to go back into your past to love the girl in you. You may have countless sexual encounters with all types of men and even interact sexually with some women, just wanting something you've missed. You don't know what it looks like, so you look everywhere—*desperate*!!! **Longing for love is a bitter pit of pain.** God desires to cut you away from the profane, wrap you in his arms, and just pour himself into you. This is why he left the Holy Spirit with us after Jesus eradicated our sin on the cross. He left the Advocate, the Comforter, the Healer, and declares that he must dwell inside of you—right where the pain resides. And as you accept this love, you evolve into a consecrated jewel in his crown because he resides in you, becoming your confidence. Yes, insecurity must leave and the ugliness dissolves. Because he lives outside of time, he touches your past, present, and future simultaneously, offering the healing power of love that creates a beautiful substance called confidence.

One of the most intriguing things about confidence that I hear in the world is found in the term "self-confidence." Really funny when you consider it from the mind-set of I Thessalonians 5:23: "May your spirit and soul and body be preserved sound *and* complete" as a result of consecration. A lot of our life trauma creating insecurity in us is a result of "self." As women, we've made some profane choices in life, and often in search of this temporal thing called "self-confidence." The Bible never makes this suggestion to find self-confidence. We are always directed to find God, because if we find the Creator then we will find our true identity, revealing who our true self is supposed to be. Let the girl in you find God's love, and your future self will find confidence and a covering.

> *Above all, love each other deeply,*
> *because love covers over a multitude of sins.*
>
> —1 PETER 4:8

[OPTION #3]
A girl becoming strong
+ a woman accepting help/support
―――――――――――――――――――――
= My Future Self

There are popular descriptions used for some women, "a strong woman" or a "strong black woman." Upon hearing either, I always get a view of an isolated woman, whether white, Asian, or black. Strong is not bad, but the connotation often promotes a sense of "I don't need anyone else." You may not *want* anyone else, but you are definitely wired to *need* other people. Remember our conversation on love? Let's see how it fits in here with strength and assistance.

> *He makes the whole body fit together perfectly.*
> *As each part does its own special work,*
> *it helps the other parts grow, so that the whole body is*
> *healthy and growing and full of love.*
>
> —EPHESIANS 4:16 *New Living Translation*

In this passage, the Apostle Paul is speaking of those of us in the Church. We are each to do our part so that we make a gorgeous collective that is… you guessed it, "full of love." There's just no way around that four-letter word. As God loves us, we are free to love others and be loved through accepting help. Maybe when you were a girl you were given a mantra that said, *"You don't need anyone, people will only hurt you! Just take care of yourself!"* Maybe it wasn't repeated to you over and over, but it was shown to you by a lonely mother or a devastated aunt. Somewhere, if you saw an isolated woman attempting to be strong, you figured being independent could shield you from disappointments and hurt. A girl who is weak believes that someone has to do things for her. She doesn't realize that she has to be involved in the process of her success. She is trained to be codependent or isolated, making more and more mistakes in life.

Handouts won't train you to walk in God's strength. I was born with what the world refers to as handicaps. My body had limitations based on its design, so I had to be taught how to overcome. This meant that as a girl, I had to see and confront my weaknesses. I couldn't live in a realm of sympathy or pity, but I did have to examine my disadvantages and turn them into advantages. I had to rise above. I had to learn different methods of walking in strength so that I'd become a woman who could accept help when needed without turning it into pity. There's a fine line between the two. The Apostle Paul wrote to both you and me telling us how he learned to grow.

> And to keep me from being puffed up and too much elated by the exceeding greatness (preeminence) of these revelations, there was given me a thorn (a splinter) in the flesh, a messenger of Satan, to rack and buffet and harass me, to keep me from being excessively exalted. Three times I called upon the Lord and besought [Him] about this and begged that it might depart from me; But He said to me, My grace (My favor and loving-kindness and mercy) is enough for you [sufficient against any danger and enables you to bear the trouble manfully]; for My strength and power are made perfect (fulfilled and completed) and show themselves most effective in [your] weakness. Therefore, I will all the more gladly glory in my weaknesses and infirmities, that the strength and power of Christ (the Messiah) may rest (yes, may pitch a tent over and dwell) upon me!
> —2 CORINTHIANS 12:7-9 *The Amplified Bible*

So Paul said that whatever brought weakness in his life, was there only to display the need for a Savior. Yes, once again salvation is showing up in our lives. So the weaknesses of life anchor us in the strength of God. We don't become strong and independent women, but we become tent dwellers! Yes, God's power is most effective when we need help. He doesn't offer us pity, but he says if I "pitch a tent" (offer a temporary dwelling so you have time to get yourself together) to cover up your inadequacy then you will be a prime candidate to display my power.

The Holy Spirit coached you into adulthood through various people and life events.

When I was 16 years old, my mother bought me a used car in desperate need of a paint job. Now, I did not pay for it with cash, but I had to earn it with inner strength. Let me explain. The car was a blueish Honda my friends and I went on to call "Born-to-Shop", because of a bumper sticker on my dashboard. I loved that car! It was cute and little and zippy. Born-to-Shop was also NOT an automatic. It was a stick shift. This meant a daily reliance on my right hand. Having three fingers on each hand, I often have more of a challenging time using my right hand.. So the night I was presented with the car, I had to address my weakness. Initially I felt my mother had made a mistake and could simply exchange the car for another (clearly I was 16 and didn't get it).

My mother gave me a 5-minute window to walk in power. It meant becoming strong, confident and allowing myself to accept her help. She set a timer for five minutes after giving me a basic 5-minute tutorial on driving a stick shift. My right hand had to coordinate with my legs. This was at a time in my life when I was still getting corrective surgeries, so my inner girl and developing woman was battling with overcoming my insecurity and my weakness in both my legs and right hand.

My mother did the quick lesson, prayed that God would walk me through it, and set the timer on the dashboard. She put me in the driver's seat, unleashed me on Kempsville Road in Virginia Beach, and I had to sink or swim or drive! She didn't guide my hand. She sat in the passenger seat and coached me through it yelling out" *"CLUTCH!" – "PULL!" – "FIGURE OUT HOW TO GET IT IN GEAR OR LOSE THE CAR!!!"* When we hit five minutes I was rolling like a warrior in my new Honda!

It was more than just earning a car; it was a girl becoming strong so I'd be a woman who could accept help without pity. When I met my husband many, many years later, as friends I had to ask him to cut my food at dinner one day since I sometimes have random difficulty in this area. This was a huge thing because it meant being vulnerable about my fingers; however, I was now a woman who could accept help. So he cut my food, and still swears that this was a defining moment of us knowing we'd be a team spending our lives in love.

Now you may not have had a mother or father, or a supportive parent. Perhaps you didn't realize it, but the Holy Spirit coached you into adulthood through various people and life events. Whatever it took, look life in the eye and say, "The power of the Messiah resides in me and his grace helps me to bear trouble womanfully!" Yell out to the air that you will succeed! Walk in it, girl! Own your life and LIVE!

COACHING QUESTIONS

Do you have a defining moment in your life when you learned to be an overcomer?

Which option will you pick, or do you need all three?

What pain and weakness did God allow in your life?

Is it hard to believe that God keeps every one of your tears?" If so, explain why.

COACHING VERSE

[PSALM 138:8 *New King James Version*]
The LORD will perfect that which concerns me;
Your mercy, O LORD, endures forever;
Do not forsake the works of Your hands.

DIVINE DECLARATION

If my success depends on how other people treat me, I will never become anything. But if I become a success in spite of this, then I have achieved a great victory. I will succeed! God is more than the world against me!

PART TWO

ANSWERS

~ CHAPTER 6 ~
Types of women

We are now embarking upon Part Two of the book that explores answers to assist in your discovery of who the Creator says you are. In this segment, let's assess what "type" you are and where you are so that as we coach you, if need be, you can make a *YOU*-turn! This will require soul honesty. It will require you looking you in the mirror. It will require the usage of God's Word.

Now let's go back to the beginning of the book, our first question: What is #girlsonamission? Remember the girl inside of you who's still very much alive? Let's examine her closely. If we're going to discover what type of woman you are, then we must get a glimpse of that girl. Let's consider four different types of women. The Bible tells an interesting account of a 12-year-old girl who many thought was dead, but Jesus said she was just asleep. This little girl was living well by most standards. She was growing up with her father, who was a man of prominence because he was a synagogue ruler, and she was at an age of discovery; nevertheless, her life was in jeopardy. There was something dangerous enough happening that her father felt he would lose her if he didn't get supernatural assistance. And so, he found Jesus.

Now when Jesus returned, a crowd welcomed him, for they were all expecting him. Then a man named

> *Jairus, a synagogue leader, came and fell at Jesus' feet, pleading with him to come to his house because his only daughter, a girl of about twelve, was dying.*
> —LUKE 8:40-42a

Amazing that in a crowd that large, her father got Jesus' attention! Wow, don't we all dream of that type of rescue? Just go to God on my behalf. Raise your voice above the crowd. Use your influence to get the Messiah to come touch me before I die. Are you that wishing woman? Are you living life helplessly, because no one helped you? Perhaps you say, "I didn't know my father; consequently, I am helpless. But if I did know him, or if he had been there…I'd be a much stronger woman."

Well, many could assume that since Jarius got Jesus' attention, all went well and there was a happy ending. BUT like many great stories, there was a huge setback. As determined and as influential as the father was, there was a delay in the little girl's healing because

---

My earthly father, Adam McFaddin, was a great businessman in the city of Los Angeles during the sixties. He had influence and power at a time when many African-American men did not.

*My mother has told the story that when I was born with all types of physical ailments; my father lifted me out of the incubator and whispered to me, "What's wrong with my little girl?" He fought for me until he couldn't fight anymore. My father died when I was three as a result of cancer. Was I left with no one to oversee my care? No, God took over from there, and I did not suffer. After an encounter with Jesus, I got up to the life purposed for me. It's been a journey, sprinkled with tears, hard work and God's love, but I am no longer **helpless**.*

of a woman in need. Yes remember, that in this crowd there was a woman who broke the law. This type of woman is what we would call **tenacious.** Although, there was no man there to help her, the man she needed was in the crowd and NOTHING would stop her. So this woman pressed on in power. This type of woman may have been sick, but she was definitely determined. This type of woman didn't stay lost in the crowd; she broke free of the crowd!

> As Jesus was on his way, the crowds almost crushed him. And a woman was there who had been subject to bleeding for twelve years, but no one could heal her. She came up behind him and touched the edge of his cloak, and immediately her bleeding stopped.
> —LUKE 8:42b-44

Everyone wants something. Let's just be real about that fact! The crowds almost crushed Jesus. Don't think that this girl and this woman were the only ones with needs. They just happened to break through. Stop letting the crowd hinder you. There will always be people in need, people praying and asking God for a blessing, and some are desperate. You have to decide that your needs will get met! I love the woman's negotiating tactic: *"If I just touch the edge of his garment!"* Yes, girl, be persistent, be unwavering, be unshakable! She assessed the crowd. She realized that Jarius was about to get his needs met, and she determined that all of Jesus was anointed...even his clothes! She decided that a "drive-by blessing" would do the job. I don't need a conversation. I just need a touch. This woman is the poster girl for tenacity! She figured, let the little girl get a sit-down, full-course blessing. I will have mine "to-go."

> *But Jesus said, "Someone touched me;*
> *I know that power has gone out from me."*
> *Then the woman, seeing that she could not go*
> *unnoticed, came trembling and fell at his feet.*
> *In the presence of all the people, she told why she*
> *had touched him and how she had been*
> *instantly healed. Then he said to her, "Daughter,*
> *your faith has healed you. Go in peace."*
>
> —LUKE 8:46-48

Uh oh, she was so focused on the goal that she forgot she was breaking the law. Why was she trembling? Because she was bleeding, iron-deficient, tired, worn-out, and quite frankly, she hadn't been around a crowd of people in a very long time...twelve years to be exact. Remember, her bleeding meant she had to be isolated. Yes, when Jarius' only daughter was being born twelve years before, this woman had to basically go into exile. Women on their monthly "cycle" were considered unclean, so they had to go outside the city until the cycle ended. But for every year Jarius' daughter grew, this woman was forced further and further into exile. Here we are, twelve years later, and it is enough for them both. Jarius' daughter got sick, and so did this woman. She got fed-up of being sick. She got sick and tired of being sick and tired! It's one thing to be sick and another to be fed up. Jarius was fed up with watching his daughter be helpless, and this woman was fed up with being helpless, too. For twelve years she spent money, went to doctors, and lived on the outskirts of everyone else's growth and development.

> **help·less** |ˈhelpləs| *adjective* **1**: unable to help oneself, powerless, vulnerable, exposed, weak or disabled
>
> **te·na·cious** |tə-ˈnā-shəs| *adjective* **1**: not readily relinquishing a position or principle or course of action, steadfast, unyielding, resolute, patient and stubborn.

What type of woman are you, helpless or tenacious? Jarius' daughter was twelve years old, and the woman had been bleeding for twelve years. Their lives intersected at the feet of Jesus. Before the woman was seized for being a law-breaker, Jesus called her "daughter" and told her to "Go in peace." I submit to you that this girl and this woman were one and the same in a way. How? Because, if you don't get your helplessness resolved as a girl, then you'll grow up to be a woman that will die if she doesn't become tenacious in her quest for Jesus.

Let's dig a little deeper into the point of intersection with the number twelve for the girl's age and the number of years the woman suffered. The number twelve represents completeness, perfect order or even God's power and authority. As a result, this account of their lives can teach us that the time of being helpless and on the brink of death is completely over. If you are either type, then you must remember who God is and the power he has. Recognize that he is the God of Peace. So this woman was told by the Prince of Peace to go in Peace, because the God of Peace put an end to her isolation, sickness and helplessness. Stop enduring the confines of helplessness because you were always told it has to be this way. You weren't created to be a helpless woman. Break through the crowd and claim what's yours. Wake up and start living!

> *While Jesus was still speaking, someone came from the house of Jarius, the synagogue leader.*
>
> *"Your daughter is dead," he said.*
>
> *"Don't bother the teacher anymore."*
>
> *Hearing this, Jesus said to Jarius, "Don't be afraid; just believe, and she will be healed."*
>
> *Meanwhile, all the people were wailing and mourning or her. "Stop wailing," Jesus said.*
>
> *"She is not dead but asleep." They laughed at him, knowing that she was dead.* 54
>
> *But he took her by the hand and said,*
>
> *"My child, get up!"*
>
> —LUKE 8:49-50, 52

After Jesus helped the woman suffering and called her daughter, Jesus now heals Jarius' daughter. He even claimed her as his own by saying "my child", and told her it was time to get up and LIVE! And I love that he told "all the people" to stop. People will declare you dead. Sometimes Jesus has to address the folks in your life. They don't know you like he knows you. He was there when you were created. He knows your purpose. He knows your destiny. He knows how he will heal you. So let him deal with your naysayers.

We could stop here, but there are still two more types of women out there hiding. Yep, there will be no lingering in the dark. I see you, and I am coming to pull you out of darkness into the light! That is the job of a true coach. So, why are you hiding? You may say, *"Well, because there is just so much to do."* You love God, but you are just trying to help him keep your life together, your family's lives together, your company's organization together, and even your church's ministry together. Isn't that what a good wife, mom, sister, boss, godmother, or team leader does? Perhaps, but not if she's trying to do what Jesus calls the "better part" in the scripture below. Oh yes, girl, if you think that you are the queen of "distracted leadership." Allow me to introduce you to two sisters:

> As Jesus and his disciples were on their way, he came to a village where a woman named Martha opened her home to him. She had a sister called Mary, who sat at the Lord's feet listening to what he said. But Martha was distracted by all the preparations that had to be made. She came to him and asked, "Lord, don't you care that my sister has left me to do the work by myself? Tell her to help me!"
>
> "Martha, Martha," the Lord answered, "You are worried and upset about many things, but few things are needed—or indeed only one. Mary has chosen what is better, and it will not be taken away from her."
>
> —LUKE 10:38-42

Have you ever had someone file a complaint on you to Jesus? Or have you ever filed a complaint on someone with Jesus? Especially in family relationships, there has probably been a time of demanding that God would come and get the house in order. One of the things that really grabbed my attention here was that Jesus was invited into their house. Your home tells so much about you. How you exist in your home environment reveals your nature. Some people try to be proper in front of company; nevertheless, when Jesus is in your house, why not take advantage and ask him to deal with the dysfunction! So, on that note, Martha decided to not be helpless but to expose her sister, even though the account says she was busy and **distracted** with preparations. Before Jesus addressed what she viewed as a problem in her sister, he told her what he saw in her, which was worry and focus on many things. That is one serious combination to becoming distracted. In fact, he called her name twice as to get her attention in the conversation.

Martha was feisty. She tried to challenge Jesus about how she felt he should respond. Those types of prayers from distracted women make me giggle. You just want the Lord to do what you think he needs to do, especially concerning you. And usually, his response to that is to do… nothing. None of us can force God's hand. One woman told my husband and me that God owed her what she was asking him for. She did not agree with how her situation was unfolding after we came and prayed with her for an answer. That actually scared me, because none of us are even owed our next breath. When my husband digested what she was saying, there came a point in the conversation where it was evident she was not budging from her stance that God didn't handle her prayer request as she thought he should. Finally, he made me get my purse and told me that our time of ministry was officially over because only God could explain the rest to her. This woman was not open to our help.

Now, Martha did one thing here that I believe saved her from being zapped by a huge angel. She didn't demand, but she exposed her frustration to Jesus in the form of a question. She wasn't so distracted that she totally forgot respect. The entire time Martha had Jesus in her midst she was busy preparing things for his visit. Mary, however, took advantage of such an illustrious houseguest and sat down right at his feet (a place of submission), **listening.** Both ladies heard from him, but not once in this passage do we hear from Mary. Are you the type of woman who knows how to **listen?** Coaching, mentoring, discipling, and pastoring you will never work if you are unable to stop and listen to godly instruction. Martha was worried, anxious, troubled, and upset. Mary was chilling. What are you doing when you talk to God?

Humor me if you will and give me a chance to share another passage about these two sisters. Take a deeper look at their personalities and interactions with Christ.

> Now a man named Lazarus was sick. He was from Bethany, the village of Mary and her sister Martha. (This Mary, whose brother Lazarus now lay sick, was the same one who poured perfume on the Lord and wiped his feet with her hair.) So the sisters sent word to Jesus, "Lord, the one you love is sick." When he heard this, Jesus said, "This sickness will not end in death. No, it is for God's glory so that God's Son may be glorified through it." Now Jesus loved Martha and her sister and Lazarus.

> *So when he heard that Lazarus was sick,*
> *he stayed where he was two more days,*
> *and then he said to his disciples,*
> *"Let us go back to Judea."*
> *When Martha heard that Jesus was coming,*
> *she went out to meet him, but Mary stayed at home.*
> *"Lord," Martha said to Jesus, "if you had been here,*
> *my brother would not have died.*
> *But I know that even now God*
> *will give you whatever you ask."*
> —JOHN 11:1-7, 20-22

It is fascinating the way Jesus interacted with this family that he loved. He was dealing with various types of people, but taught them all in one magnificent way. Sometimes the difficulty your family is going through isn't all about you, but Jesus is loving all of you and teaching all of you simultaneously. Don't just look through the lens of how situations affect you. You have to be patient with the way problems are solved, how prayers are answered, and how the Lord sends help to everyone.

Firstly, we find that they agreed that Jesus' help was needed. Agreement is always critical to breakthrough, because there is power in agreement. Secondly, the scripture says that Mary was the one who had anointed and wiped his feet, showing you that she was a woman of abandoning worship. She gave her all. Later, John points out that Jesus loved all three of them, but only named Martha and Lazarus, not their sister, Mary. John was very tied to the heart of Jesus, so he examined the agape that Christ showed others. I believe he wanted us to be clear in his account, that even though Martha had to be corrected, she was definitely loved by Jesus.

In addition, because of the love Jesus had for them, he delayed their miracle. *Wait, what?!* That's how you show love??? You stay away??? When he finally did arrive, Martha got so **distracted** again by her family's need that she didn't even let him come inside, but went out into the streets to tell him her thoughts. Then, she followed up her controlling style with *"but I know…"* It was as if she wanted him to see that she was trying to break free from her administrative mind to focus on the fact that whenever he arrived, he'd still make things all right, but she was hurting. John, the writer, also mentioned that Mary stayed at home. I love that girl; she still hasn't said a word! Mary's heart said, "I've spent a lot of time worshipping and listening to him, now all I have to do is watch him work!" Remember, **listening** is how you build relationship.

> **dis·tract·ed** |disˈtraktəd| *adjective* **1**: unable to concentrate because one's mind is preoccupied, out of one's head, inattentive, harassed
>
> **lis·ten·ing** |ˈlis(ə)niŋ | *verb* **1**: taking notice of and acting on what someone says; responding to advice or a request; giving one's attention to a sound

What type of woman are you? **Distracted** or **listening,** both take action. A distracted woman, however, uses so much energy that she really cannot think. To be a woman of substance, you need to keep your mind stayed on Christ. A listening woman takes time to give something her full and undivided attention and responds accordingly. A listening woman must walk in serious power, because she has to be able to address properly all she is encountering. This is why talking will often interfere with her being able to do the exact thing needed.

Okay, that lesson is over. You have four options to choose from: helpless, tenacious, distracted or listening. You can pick more than one, and you can also distinguish between who you currently are and who you plan to become. Just be sure to listen and let the Lord guide your answer.

CHAPTER QUESTIONS

Is there comfort in the lack of responsibility when feeling like you are helpless and if so, explain?

What is the greatest difficulty in being "every woman": friend, sister, mother, daughter, boss, employee, wife, etc.

How have the changes, problems and adjustments you've had in your life isolated you or taken over your existence? Explain.

COACHING VERSE

[ISAIAH 26:3 *New Living Translation*]
You will keep in perfect peace all who trust in you,
all whose thoughts are fixed on you!

DIVINE DECLARATION

Dear Lord, I want to be a woman that listens and worships you. I want to know when to push forward and when to lean on you. Balance me and make me over. May the God of Peace send the Prince of Peace to give me perfect Peace.

CHAPTER 7
Types of goals

As we continue on in the project development of YOU, let us consider another question. If you had to capture in one word, what your ultimate goal is in life, what would it be? Give it some thought. In fact, how about you fill in the blank below but don't rush. May I suggest that you actually set the book down and reflect on your answer? We're talking about using one word to define your focus.

My goal is: _____.

Hi there, glad you are back. What did you write? Notice I didn't give you a lot of room. I wanted you to be concise. These one-word goals to be discussed will be referred to as "umbrella words," because they are a broad stroke for a lot of the activity you will fulfill. Now, if you were unable to define your goal, it is okay. Let's continue. I know you could probably recite several goals; so, as your coach, I will present three options to start your speculating about this question. We all have goals. A goal is your life aim or the desired result for why you live. It is the ultimate object of all your striving, ambition, and efforts. It is your reason to work hard. So now that we've narrowed down the type of woman you want to be, we must also consider what type of goal this woman should have.

I believe goals wake you up in the morning. I believe that without a reason for being, you move slowly, live aimlessly, and feel insignificant. Ultimately, if you don't have a goal, you tend to waste time. We must be aware of time and how to best invest it. Even if we're just playing

> *Some goals are career-driven, some are for personal advancement, and others are for the betterment of our world.*

with a child or cooking a meal for a husband or going to school, we must see it as part of a bigger plan and advancing toward our goal. Some goals are career-driven, some are for personal advancement, and others are for the betterment of our world.

No matter the category, most of the time, our goals can be placed under the umbrella of one word that drives our focus. Many Christians will state their goal while trying to stay "religiously correct." They may even use one of the following types of words: Jesus, church, service, or evangelism. And for many, this may be an accurate assessment for their life goals. I even have to admit, pretty much all I do can be placed under the Ministry goal. I'm about service, so if what I'm doing doesn't serve, then I'm falling short of my life goal mark. Many of these "religiously correct" words are typical umbrella words for all of our goals. Therefore I want to suggest that you to look a little deeper. It's okay; I've cleared it with God for us to use non-Christianese. But be warned, my coaching agenda may expose you to your authentic self.

It's only logical that if it's your goal, then it's always about pleasing you and making you happy. That's fair, right? Isn't it about getting richer, popular, skinnier, and any other word that will bring the self-focus to the forefront of your entire life agenda? Honestly, a lot of our goals are about getting to a place where we'll finally be a part of the "club" so we can hang with the cool chicks, the noticed crew and the glittering girlfriends. I mean, let's be transparent. If this is just a conversation between us, then can't you admit that piece of truth to your coach? If so, then repeat this line: "My goal is to just be really cool." Ha! You admitted it. Listen, assuming you were you the underdog, the forgotten girl, the head of the unpopular club in high school you probably would set a goal to do all in your power to feed your **Ego.** Right? Let's say you weren't the underdog; maybe you were "most likely to…" As a result, you set the goal of maintaining your status in the world and purposed in your heart to maintain your Ego at all cost, but an unscheduled decision or relationship may have set you back a bit in the steps you took to bring about this reality. Did you become a wife or mom sooner than planned, so you had to put all of your dreams on the back burner? Now that everyone took your time, got your focus, and cost you some dreams, you just may want to be a woman who can finally focus on her Ego … in peace?

> **e·go** |ˈēgō| *noun* **1**: a person's sense of self-esteem or self-importance

It is the sum of your self-confidence, self-worth, self-image, and self-respect. So if Ego is your goal, then it only makes sense that your entire drive and passion is about you. Well, you wouldn't be the first person to set that goal, but what a big umbrella to carry! Sometimes big is good, but in this case big is overwhelmingly steeped in arrogance. Being arrogant means you have an exaggerated sense of your own importance or ability. And exaggerated leaves very little room for God, and the love of God, which requires that we focus on other people. Consequently, this causes the pursuit of Ego to lead you off course, away from fulfilling God's purpose for your life. It may be hard to grasp, but even when God walked this earth in the person of Jesus Christ, he had to ditch his Ego. If you can't fathom how to make this happen, this scripture is a good place to start.

> Do nothing out of selfish ambition or vain conceit.
> Rather, in humility value others above yourselves,
> not looking to your own interests but each of you
> to the interests of the others.
> In your relationships with one another,
> have the same mindset as Christ Jesus:
> Who, being in very nature God,
> did not consider equality with God something
> to be used to his own advantage;
> rather, he made himself nothing
> by taking the very nature of a servant,
> being made in human likeness.
> And being found in appearance as a man,
> he humbled himself
> by becoming obedient to death—
> even death on a cross!
>
> —PHILIPPIANS 2:3-8

Remember that in all of our getting, we must constantly leave room for God's will and purpose for our lives. The Ego goal says I have to focus on self, so I can't focus on others or even God. This is why Christians with an Ego goal have a unique view of prayer. It is a tool, but not a communion. If Ego is your goal, then prayer is full of requests and lists. You are constantly seeking the hands of the Lord instead of the Lord himself. You don't have time to build relationship with the Lord, because getting your needs met is the top priority. And if you don't get to cross something off your list, then God is not worthy of worship. Clearly when it's all about you, there's no time for worship anyway. Your interaction with God is legalistic and technical; therefore, worship makes absolutely no sense. Worship is intimate and revealing for both you and the Lord. Every now and then you can tap in if a song or lyric points to your needs being met, other than that, you'll just pop into church for the message all the while praying it feeds your Ego. *"Singing keeps me from getting the advice I need to fulfill the Ego goal I've set. And why get distracted by loving God when I'm too busy loving myself. Right?"*

This Ego goal actually opposes godly principles, and it contradicts another umbrella word – **People.** Whether it's career, personal, or based upon your worldview, setting the People goal will keep you aligned with Christ in two very powerful ways: humility and meekness. Before discussing those two ways, let's go back and review and dissect the same passage we just read.

> Do nothing out of selfish ambition or vain conceit. Rather, in humility value others above yourselves, not looking to your own interests but each of you

> to the interests of the others.
> In your relationships with one another,
> have the same mindset as Christ Jesus:
> Who, being in very nature God,
> did not consider equality with God something
> to be used to his own advantage;
> rather, he made himself nothing
> by taking the very nature of a servant,
> being made in human likeness.
> And being found in appearance as a man,
> he humbled himself
> by becoming obedient to death—
> even death on a cross!
>
> —PHILIPPIANS 2:3-8

Isn't that totally encouraging? If you were to look through the lens of this self-absorbed culture, it actually sounds like a definite path to a not-so-fortune 500 company! It even sounds like a perfect way to decrease your social media following, even if you have set the People goal. People are attracted to power. In this era, do people only "follow" you if you are proud and ego-driven? Well, God flips that script, and takes you counter-culture in your quest to name your umbrella goal.

Regardless of what any non-believer or atheist says, no one can argue against one of the most powerful world figures of all time, Jesus. I purposely called him a "world figure" because I'm speaking from the point of view of those who don't follow him as Lord of all. I met a

Muslim once who told me: "Jesus was a mighty prophet." I responded, "No, Jesus is the mighty God." Jesus Christ is quoted by many religions and studied in history by those who still don't agree that he's the Way, the Truth, and the Life, by which no one can come to God outside of him (John 14:6). So if someone chooses to not believe Jesus is the Messiah, they cannot argue that he is one of the most popular figures of all time. His death actually rules our calendar. Whatever year we claim it to be. We're marking the moment he died on Calvary (AD – After Death, Anno Domini-in the year of our Lord, and BC – (Before Christ). There is now an attack on these references as society has switched to BCE (before common era) and CE (common era). This is an attempt to strip any reference to the belief that Jesus is Lord. Nevertheless, the BCE and CE distinction is still based on the life of Christ. So call it what you will, the Lord is still in control.

If I simply refuse to say he's the King of Kings (as the Bible states he is in Revelation 17:14) and see him as nothing more than a prominent figure, I would still be able to read the previous passage and pull out the following via Jesus' life example:

GOD'S 5-POINT PLAN FOR WALKING IN POWER:
1. Do nothing out of selfish ambition.
2. In humility, value others above yourself.
3. Do not use your advantages to dominate others.
4. Take on the nature of a servant.
5. Humble yourself and die on a cross.

Jesus did the above five things and has more "followers" than the world has ever known. He was never accepted by the religious regime at that time. He was beaten and didn't fight back. He was a prime example of someone setting a People goal. So no matter how you slice it, if you want to be successful, follow Christ. You can't do it unless you ditch the "self" focus of Ego and cling to humility and meekness in order to genuinely pull it off. Being humble and meek will require that you don't see People as followers or fans. If you recall Jesus always had a crowd waiting for him, looking for him or meeting him. Consider what he said about the crowds.

> When he saw the crowds, he had compassion on them,
> because they were harassed and helpless,
> like sheep without a shepherd.
>
> —MATTHEW 9:36

That, unfortunately and fortunately, was the focus of Palm Sunday; the crowd cheered him on that day. But if you keep reading, they quickly had a change of heart and killed him the following week. So please consider not making followers a key part of your focus (I'm just saying). If you only see followers and fans, then you won't be able to recognize harassed and helpless People; as a result you won't be able to walk in power. Assuming you have set the People goal, then you must have realized that each person in the crowd has a specific need. If you're going to meet that need, then it will require you to walk in this 5-point plan of power more than ever. With that in mind, you definitely achieve the People goal if you cling to humility and meekness. How do they apply? You ask simply fabulous questions. Here's how:

hu·mil·i·ty |(h)yoo'milədē| *noun*
1: refers to your attitude towards yourself,
a low estimate of your importance.

> **meek·ness** |ˈmēknis| *noun* **1**: restraining
> one's power in order to allow room for others.

So humility has an inward-focus, and meekness an outward-focus. Humility says, whatever I want may get in the way of what someone else may need. Meekness asks, how can I make sure others have an opportunity to bloom and flourish? That was the power of Jesus' submission to going to Calvary. Consider his powerful prayer before the process of the Passion began.

> He went a little farther and fell on His face,
> and prayed, saying, "O My Father,
> if it is possible, let this cup pass from Me;
> nevertheless, not as I will, but as You will."
>
> —MATTHEW 26:39

How do you pray a prayer like this when you are in complete agony? When the goal of People is your umbrella, you must forget about the pain attached to bearing your cross in order to conquer death for their benefit and freedom from pain. That is why you must be both humble and meek. Please note that there are several avenues by which you can get free, bona fide training in this area: work, marriage, parenting, and more. Anywhere you must interact with people up close and personal, you're being trained in humility and meekness. And as your coach, I submit to you that one method sharpens the other.

Once when I was living in Atlanta, a friend from California came to visit me, she was overjoyed to share about her recent engagement to be married. Her focus was all over the place, as she was quite distracted by the blinding light of this romantic fantasy. You know, planning a wedding can totally distract you from being married, because your attention is more focused on the one day, as opposed to the entire rest of your life. So before she left, I asked her to go with me to walk my dogs, Peace and Joy. They were affectionately known as "the girls" and had a reputation with many. I have so many amazing stories of our adventures together. I miss them terribly to this day. Those furry, reddish-brown chows were with me for 14 glorious years.

We grabbed the leashes and our tennis shoes, the four of us ventured out for a walk. Of course, we talked about marriage, and I used the walk as a time to coach. Very casually, I gave my friend a little green waste bag as she walked one dog and I walked the other. As she enjoyed the cardio of the brisk walk, the girls suddenly stopped to relieve themselves. My friend gabbed away about her plans while the girls did their business. I interrupted her and said, "Just use the bag." Her facial expression said, "For what?" My response was that this was the best form of marriage counseling: "learning how to pick up poop!" Yep, you want the glitter, but you have to take the poop, too. After the wedding, the tux will come off and the relationship will require the daily grind of poop. Why? Because people up close and personal poop on your green grass! Oh yes, my darling girl… you have a vision of the romance and perfect union, but never forget that our vision is often controlled by fantasy. The poop reminds you that life is real and often stinks, but clean up the messes and throw them away!

Twitter, Facebook, Instagram, and even Pinterest followers will love you until you get real! Make a comment stating that you don't believe in same-sex marriage, or a particular politician, or a transgender popular personality, or that you believe society should take another approach to the roles in marriage and dissolve itself of all reality shows that begin with The Housewives of… and you will need to get out those baggies, because the poop will definitely start flying! And if you approach this from a non-humble and not so meek place, you would have wasted your time, because the followers and fans wouldn't be able to see love and compassion in your reasoning. This will let you know if it was really about followers for vainglory, and you will be sobbing in three hours as all your "crowd" drops you and runs over to someone that tickles their fancy. If you had a People goal and you wanted to offer followers godly insight and a ray of hope for change and redemption, then you may be sobbing; but it will be because you are moved with compassion as you weave your message with the fabric of love.

Lastly, there's one fun little goal that must be mentioned, just in case the Ego or People goal ran right past you and went over your head. I must ask you if your ultimate umbrella goal in life is for Stuff.

> *"Love may cost you your favorite sweater or a vital organ, and you'll never know which one when you sign up."*

Yep, there's such a thing as a **Stuff** goal. It's quite funny, because I actually was going to use the term *trinkets,* but that speaks of a tiny object with low value, and I know that many of you place a high value on big Stuff! Boy, I'll tell you, #GIRLSONAMISSION has a study called "Declutter Your Soul." I was completely humbled to learn the first day I presented it at our Bloom session that whether Stuff is tangible or intangible, people don't like you talking about their irrational or unhealthy attachment to Stuff! This wasn't the most popular lesson I've ever done, but oh so necessary. You're welcome to download the lessons from our website. This will let us know if you can tolerate my coaching, because the study causes us to address a lot of life Stuff. (But that's probably another book.)

Anyway, back to the Stuff goal conversation. People want to own things, stuff, and property, it's just built into our fleshly DNA. Somewhere along the way, many believe Stuff will protect them if their job ends, if a famine hits the land or if they desire to be buried in a huge, gigantic coffin. I'm sure you've seen the bumper sticker that states: "Whoever dies with the most stuff, wins!" We're not sure what you win, but it speaks of the competitive nature of the flesh. The Stuff goal screams that your identity is found in what you own. If you have a paid-for Toyota, it just isn't as comforting as a leased BMW with a $679 monthly payment. You're about to throw the book away, because my next statement may speak to your favorite things. But this is why television and social media can be so bad for your spirit. It strips you of proper focus, because your worldview becomes shaped completely by those with Stuff and those without Stuff.

I'm just informing you that stuff can't save you or anyone else! For example, when you become obsessed with holding on to stuff, you become a hoarder. Hoarding is a direct result of fear. The person who longs to have a lot of stuff and makes this their life focus will never find satisfaction or love. Love only works when it's an action verb. The action of loving causes you to give. One minister told my mother once, *"Love may cost you your favorite sweater or a vital organ, and you'll never know which one when you sign up."*

> As he went out into the street,
> a man came running up,
> greeted him with great reverence, and asked,
> "Good Teacher, what must I do to get eternal life?"
> Jesus said, "Why are you calling me good?
> No one is good, only God.
> You know the commandments: Don't murder,
> don't commit adultery, don't steal, don't lie,
> don't cheat, honor your father and mother."
> He said, "Teacher, I have—from my youth—
> kept them all!"
> Jesus looked him hard in the eye—and loved him!
> He said, "There's one thing left:
> Go sell whatever you own and give it to the poor.
> All your wealth will then be heavenly wealth.
> And come follow me."
> The man's face clouded over.
> This was the last thing he expected to hear,
> and he walked off with a heavy heart.
> He was holding on tight to a lot of things,
> and not about to let go.
>
> —MARK 10:17-22

What about you? Have you set a Stuff goal? How many pairs of Jimmy Choo shoes do you just HAVE TO HAVE? What type of car will you drive? What is the only carat diamond you will accept upon a marriage proposal? Ask yourself if you are like the Rich Young Ruler, "Holding on tight to a lot of things...and not about to let go." You may not even have all the stuff you want yet, but because that's your goal, you will die if you don't achieve it. You are obsessed and cannot think around what you want, so you will just fall apart if you don't get what you want. Because of this, you don't tithe give offerings in church, or help friends in need, because you cannot jeopardize your stuff budget. You have to protect your façade and image of illusion no matter who says, "Follow me."

One way to keep your—SELF in check is to give away something you like every now and then. I attended a woman's conference last year and during lunch I proceeded to enter a crowded restroom. Standing in line, a woman complimented my earrings and said they were very pretty. I simply said thank you as I entered the stall. Coming out I saw her washing her hands. As quickly as possible, I took off my earrings and gave them to the woman. She almost passed out. I didn't linger for fear of her compliments stroking my ego. It was a moment where the power of humility and meekness pushed my People goal to the surface in order to stamp out any possible hint of Stuff and Ego. If you are looking for a cool replacement, consider the umbrella word, Service. It's a glorious goal to pick up once you ditch the Stuff goal. Be like Jesus, your Savior and rock, utilize the **God's 5-point plan for walking in power.** It may take a lifetime but it's so fulfilling. As gorgeous as you are, why not possess a brilliant, dazzling, exquisite, impressive, lovely, luxurious goal? Cheering for you, your coach on the sidelines.

CHAPTER QUESTIONS

What's one thing you love that you could give away right now?

Which point of the 5-point plan for walking in power, would do you the most good?

What's one of your main ways of serving in life?

COACHING VERSE

[MATTHEW 6:33]
But seek first his kingdom and his righteousness, and all these things will be given to you as well.

[MATTHEW 6:33 *The Message Bible*]
Steep your life in God-reality, God-initiative, God-provisions. Don't worry about missing out. You'll find all your everyday human concerns will be met.

DIVINE DECLARATION

Dear Lord, I want YOU. Dear Lord, I need YOU. Help me decrease so you can increase in me.

CHAPTER 8
Types of success

We're almost to the finish line of completing the book. But before all of that, there are a few more steps to get you prepared to begin to release that fabulous potential that resides on the inside. Many are simply looking for coaching in order to be successful in business. Everyone wants to wear that life label – SUCCESS. It is the bank account, the dream house, the 2.5 kids and the white picket fence… and don't forget the fully loaded SUV in the circular driveway. Success is such a major word that both the world and Christendom lay claim to it, because everyone wants to be successful at how they learn, what they do, and who they are. And as your coach, I want you to be clear on what you consider success to mean. Is it acquiring a Swiss bank account and property in three states? Or maybe it's employing a nanny to raise your 2.5 children and having a husband that has a private jet to fly him to his offices overseas?

> **suc·cess** |səkˈses| *noun* **1**: attainment of a higher social status; the attainment of popularity or profit; or the achieving of a goal or academic accomplishment. resolute, patient and stubborn

For many it is having that "Hollywood ending," as the Oxford American Writer's Thesaurus stated. Yes, success was actually reduced down to how a fake Hollywood movie ends its script as though everyone on screen trots off with never ending joy. Consider this Bible verse that speaks of prosperity and the fullness of success.

> Beloved, I pray that you may prosper in every way and [that your body] may keep well, even as [I know] your soul keeps well and prospers. In fact, I greatly rejoiced when [some of] the brethren from time to time arrived and spoke [so highly] of the sincerity and fidelity of your life, as indeed you do live in the Truth [the whole Gospel presents]. I have no greater joy than this, to hear that my [spiritual] children are living their lives in the Truth.
> —3 JOHN 1:2-4 *The Amplified Bible*

I love that John, a church elder, is sending this out to Gaius, whom he is coaching or has coached. In verse 2 he is telling the coached how he's been praying for him regarding prosperity and success. While in verse 4 the coach gives a glimpse of how he views part of his own success and prosperity. Funny, John never speaks of Gaius' material possessions (bank accounts or automobiles or other external stuff), but he speaks of two critical components that make up who Gaius is: body and soul. If these two components are in place, then a lot of the *Stuff* you desire will come in time. His body represents being in good health, and his soul represents balanced thoughts, emotions, and actions. It is evident that his spirit success is evident, because in verse 3 it states that many have reported that he walks in fidelity, the whole

You can be a public success and a private failure.

Gospel, and the truth of God. His coach prayed for Gaius' success to be found in the balance of his entire being: body, soul, and spirit.

From a coaching perspective, let's consider a few new questions: What does inner success look like? And how can we achieve it? It appears that many books line the shelves teaching on outer success by getting more money, gaining a solid education, and mastering the golden career. But what do you do when you've gained those things, but you live in inner turmoil without inner success? My mother says that you can be a public success and a private failure. So I ask, how do we avoid the latter? What does inner success look like? How do we reach for a balanced person as John spoke over Gaius? Let's uncover two steps to inner success that protect the inward and outward expression of honor.

The first way to ensure inner triumph is to gain **spiritual success**. Remember that there are three components that make you a whole person. Our soul is the middleman being strengthened or lured by either our spirit or our body. God and Satan both seek to claim your soul. Satan uses his influence over your body through the door of your senses: sight, taste, touch, sound and smell. God uses his influence over your spirit through the power of being part of a church body that teaches you about who he is, reading his word, listening to godly music and surrounding yourself with godly people. Soul influence is all about the greatest deposited made by either your spirit or body. When we accept Christ as our Savior, he saves our soul: mind, emotions, and our will. But Satan seeks to control this part of you in order to maintain torment, by stealing, killing, and destroying the essence of who you are. Let us find an anchor in spiritual success so that Satan will have to loosen his grip of control. If we do want a wonderful career and advanced academic achievement, all leading to financial prosperity, then there should be a focus on how to sustain these desires so that we don't get it and get got! God must be able to pour life into your spirit so that you have divine direction on what is really for you.

The Bible was ultimately written for our spiritual success, so it's packed with an outpouring of truth for our spiritual success and development. There are two scriptural references that we'll focus on for this coaching exercise. If you stick with me for the next steps of spiritual development and become mentored, discipled or pastored, then you will learn, study, and discover a lot more to grow you into a successfull force to be reckoned with by Satan and his representatives.

> So get rid of all evil behavior. Be done with all deceit,
> hypocrisy, jealousy, and all unkind speech.
> Like newborn babies,
> you must crave pure spiritual milk
> so that you will grow into a full experience of salvation.
> Cry out for this nourishment, now that you have
> had a taste of the Lord's kindness.
> —1 PETER 2:1-3 *New Living Translation*

> **THIS SCRIPTURE INVOLVES THE REMOVAL OF INTERNAL ERRORS IN YOUR SPIRIT:**
>
> ### Evil Behavior
> Wicked actions and depravity
>
> ### Deception
> Cheating & feelings of hatred
>
> ### Hypocrisy
> Dishonesty, being two-faced
>
> ### Jealousy
> Possessiveness, suspiciousness
>
> ### Slander
> Talking about people to others or speaking negatively to them

These are the five errors, which rob you of a truly successful life. After you remove the errors, you will then crave (beg for, desire, hunger for, dream of, and yearn for) a new diet. This new diet begins with undiluted spiritual milk to help you grow in salvation and a full experience of Christ taking over the management of your soul. Once your spirit gets used to spiritual milk, then you can move on to the meat of God's word. By removing these internal errors, you take your spirit back to your beginning, to the newborn place where your learning began. This is why the Bible says in John 3 that you must be born again. Removing errors to gain spiritual success requires a dying to self. The only way to get spiritual milk inside of you is to experience rebirth.

Working towards spiritual success means you are willing to do something new to gain a desired result. Most successful people would think that you only get ahead in life by using these five errors: evil behavior, deception, hypocrisy, jealousy, and slander. But God calls you to live counter to the culture and lean on his salvation once you taste and experience his kindness. As you learn more about him by strengthening your spirit, God's love and kindness will eliminate a desire to live according to these methods. Put your spirit on a "holy milk" diet! It will purge out a lot of junk that may give you outside achievement, but no inner success. With inner success you can sleep at night knowing that integrity and uprightness guided your actions. These are powerful coaching steps that train you to be a #girlonamission who is success-full and prosperous.

> Whatever happens, conduct yourselves in a manner worthy of the gospel of Christ. Then, whether I come and see you or only hear about you in my absence, I will know that you stand firm in the one Spirit, striving together as one for the faith of the gospel without being frightened in any way by those who oppose you. This is a sign to them that they will be destroyed, but that you will be saved—and that by God.
>
> —PHILIPPIANS 1:27-28

Now this scripture speaks of a connection to a coach or mentor. It is an instruction given that is set up to keep you going even if you don't have someone there holding your hand. It is a command that will continue throughout your lifetime. This speaks of fulfilling your mission. If you feel as though you're life path is being guided to achieve something greater than working a job, but is a mission that you are called to accomplish in the earth, then learn these two powerful phrases: first,

> In order for you to assess the power of your salvation, tough experiences need to occur to train you.

whatever happens; and second, *conduct yourselves.* When the Holy Spirit resides on the inside of you, he fills the places that used to house those five internal errors; therefore, your conduct changes no matter how you are tested. The holy milk diet sets you on a new road, and you will be tested. This is when phrase #1 comes into play:whatever happens. In order for you to assess the power of your salvation, tough experiences need to occur to train you. You have no control over what happens in your life; your job is to just be ready *whatever happens.*

Your initial response, in any situation you may encounter after removing those internal errors and being filled with the Holy Spirit, is to conduct yourself in a manner worthy of the gospel of Christ. And this requires knowing the gospel of Christ. Inner triumph doesn't become official until you show your spiritual success through conduct. Many people claim Christ, but they don't know how to conduct themselves like him when hit with their "whatevers." No matter what, you have to represent Jesus, because your coach may not always be there at your disposal, but may only hear about your conduct (reread Philippians 1:27). But those guiding your spiritual development in any of the four categories need to know that you are standing firm; that you are thriving with others, and are not frightened by opposition of any kind to your faith. These trainers are never successful until the student becomes unyielding in the face of opposition. If you are being coached or disciple into a new life in Christ, then you need to exemplify the powerful training you have received. Remember, John had to hear that Gaius was standing for the Truth in the face of "whatever happens."

The spiritual component covered the first part of this inner victory, but now let's take a look at the second part…**relational success.** This is why conduct is key, because relationships of all kinds reveal how spiritually successful you really are. The unexpected events in life that will test your conduct will more than likely involve other people and relationships. Yes, relationships are our ultimate test for success. Interconnectedness is the measuring rod for the removal of internal errors.

> Beloved, I implore you as aliens and strangers and exiles
> [in this world] to abstain from the sensual urges
> (the evil desires, the passions of the flesh,
> your lower nature) that wage war against the soul.
> Conduct yourselves properly (honorably, righteously)
> among the Gentiles, so that, although
> they may slander you as evildoers,
> [yet] they may by witnessing

> *your good deeds [come to] glorify God in the day of inspection [when God shall look upon you wanderers as a pastor or shepherd looks over his flock].*
>
> —1 PETER 2:11-12

In order to ensure our relational success, we must use the springboard from our spiritual success and conduct ourselves properly among those who believe differently. This time we must start with expelling outward errors found in sensual and emotional urges of the flesh, or body, because they attack your soul. Remember, the fight is all about your soul (thoughts, emotions and actions), and the body pulls on the soul just like our spirit does. So if you are to be full of inner success, then you have to ensure that your body doesn't have control of your soul. People, possessing their own internal errors, may lie and accuse you because they don't have the same spiritual conviction as you do; nevertheless, also realize that your humble response and control of anger will be seen by them with the hopes that they, too, will glorify God.

> *Bear with each other and forgive one another if any of you has a grievance against someone. Forgive as the Lord forgave you. And over all these virtues put on love, which binds them all together in perfect unity.*
>
> —COLOSSIANS 3:13-14

Once people see that you use godly principles to gain control of your thoughts, emotions and actions, they will have to acknowledge your conduct. (Keep in mind, they may be too arrogant to admit to it.) You have to maneuver with spirit-driven steps to ensure relational success. That is walking in the power of outward expression by bearing with and forgiving others no matter what happens. You know that you've been forgiven, so now you must repeat these steps toward others so you can experience the power of relational success.

Dress in virtue. These virtues are bound together by the Lord living in you and covering you. The definition of virtue is that which helps us bear with people and forgive in our relationships. It is power. Being virtuous breeds powerful living. People of this power are successful, spiritually and relationally. So whether they are millionaires with several luxury cars or live in a modest home and drive a used car, they are operating in inner success. They are able to experience divine access to the God of Hope, the God of Peace, and most importantly, the God who is Love. Are you ready to enjoy inner success with godly balance in your mind, emotions and actions?

CHAPTER QUESTIONS

What type of success have you always desired?

In what specific ways can your life bloom with spiritual and relational success?

Which internal errors have had the greatest impact in your life? Explain.

COACHING VERSE

[1 TIMOTHY 6:6-10 *The Amplified Bible*]
[And it is, indeed, a source of immense profit, for] godliness accompanied with contentment (that contentment which is a sense of [a]inward sufficiency) is great *and* abundant gain.

For we brought nothing into the world, and *obviously* we cannot take anything out of the world; But if we have food and clothing, with these we shall be content (satisfied).

But those who crave to be rich fall into temptation and a snare and into many foolish (useless, godless) and hurtful desires that plunge men into ruin *and* destruction and miserable perishing.

For the love of money is a root of all evils; it is through this craving that some have been led astray *and* have wandered from the faith and pierced themselves through with many [b]acute [mental] pangs.

[PROVERBS 30:7-9 *New Living Translation*]
O God, I beg two favors from you; let me have them before I die.
First, help me never to tell a lie.
Second, give me neither poverty nor riches!
Give me just enough to satisfy my needs.
For if I grow rich, I may deny you and say, "Who is the LORD?"
And if I am too poor, I may steal and thus insult God's holy name.

DIVINE DECLARATION

Lord, although I desire things ultimately, I am driven to possess inward sufficiency through godly living. Bless me according to your unlimited resources deposited in my inner woman.

_____
_____
_____
_____
_____
_____
_____
_____
_____
_____
_____
_____
_____

CHAPTER 9
Types of prayer

Let's consider your goals and what success looks like for you. In order to do that, we must first examine prayer, for without it, nothing in this coaching relationship is possible. Presently, I am challenged by a new commitment in our church, to host a weekly prayer call for women every Wednesday morning at 6:00am. It would be great for you to join us! (Information is under the Resource section of the book.) Many desire to pray for something; however, my calling is to help women build a devoted relationship with the Lord, then all the Stuff will follow. Presenting prayer requests must not be our number one agenda in prayer, even though we are instructed to ask. Prayer requests are best presented as you establish a relationship and know yourself as a friend of God… and as his daughter. This happens when you commune and study and worship him. Let's dig in!

To become a woman of effective prayer, you must endeavor to present yourself as a girl. People tend to approach relationships from a place of past experiences. They are more often than not guarded. Girls, however, are usually untainted, and approach with abandonment because they don't have past experiences. They talk openly, love freely and want to know about the people around them. They do this by asking questions to understand character, and they don't mind spending extended time with those they like.

As we grow into womanhood, we experience let down, hurt,

betrayal and broken trust, because the world is not perfect and neither are people. We build relationships with a shield over our hearts. In addition to gaining access to uncomfortable experiences, we grow up and get busy building a life, which limits our availability to spend quality time on most relationships. There are meetings, work, events, family needs and more. But to build our relationship with the Lord, we must put down our heart shield and invest real time. Finding this time to commune with God is a challenge for me too, because there's always something going on in life. But when I break away from what has to be done, I find myself enjoying the Lord in a phenomenal man-

> *Prayer affords me the opportunity to minimize my womanhood so that the girl in me can be refreshed and rejuvenated.*

ner. I find that there's even redemption of my time, and I gain divine understanding of how to proceed with all of my events, commitments and relationships. God can actually free up your time with his counsel. Prayer affords me the opportunity to minimize my womanhood so that the girl in me can be refreshed and rejuvenated. When she spends time with her Father, the woman in me finds her peace and begins to hope again. When I hope, then I'm more equipped to ask God for anything, because I'm now aligned with his Spirit so I desire what was originally intended for me when I was created. Every father wants to give his children the best. And this becomes evident when you spend time in prayer focused on relationship building. When you are hiding from intimacy and not connected to your Source, your prayers are short and requests mundane, finite, and inferior in nature; therefore, you won't want to make the investment in prayer, because that type is not inviting or refreshing.

With all that being laid out, let us ask more questions and discover types of prayer. How must we pray to be consecrated in our relationship with the Lord? How must we pray to be effective in our mission? These are the questions that should drive your focus. We will examine three types of prayers that should be adopted into your relationship with the Lord. Okay, let's just jump into the deep end of the pool and work our way to more shallow waters. The first and one of the most intense forms of prayer is **supplication**, which speaks of heavy petitioning or begging for something earnestly.

> Be anxious for nothing, but in everything by prayer and supplication, with thanksgiving,
> Let your requests be made known to God;
> and the peace of God, which surpasses all understanding, will guard your hearts and minds through Christ Jesus.
>
> —PHILIPPIANS 4:6-7 *New King James Version*

> And the Holy Spirit helps us in our weakness. For example, we don't know what God wants us to pray for. But the Holy Spirit prays for us with groanings

> that cannot be expressed in words.
> And the Father who knows all hearts
> knows what the Spirit is saying,
> for the Spirit pleads for us believers[L]
> in harmony with God's own will.
>
> —ROMANS 8:26-27 *New Living Translation*

You may recall the account of Hannah praying for a son (1 Samuel 1:9-18). As she prayed at the temple, her supplication seemed as though she was a drunk woman because of her intense overwhelming begging before the Lord. She was laid out wailing in the temple. Finally the man of God told her to get up, because her desire would be given to her.

When you arrive at the supplication level during prayer, you are completely desperate! You need God so badly, that there's no formality at all. You just drop to your knees and begin to petition him with all of your being! Often enough, you can be so overwhelmed that the Holy Spirit will step in and politely take over all your words and crying. When he enters the equation, there are no earthly words exchanged between you and the Almighty Lord...just mumbling, groaning, and crying out. This is where the church is often split, because groaning can be called praying in the Spirit or speaking in tongues. Some do not want to believe tongues is another language, (a heavenly language, if you will) so they ignore this. Let's avoid a debate, and just say if you've ever had to desperately petition God with ALL you have... you won't care if it's groaning, unknown words, or English—just *take me to the King*! Now, as your coach, I do want to say that I believe in speaking in tongues. I believe that the Holy Spirit knows the language of heaven, and that it shields the deepest requests from Satan and even blocks out our doubtful thoughts. I believe that speaking in tongues, cuts off the fat and gets straight to the meat of communicating and asking the Lord for his will to be done for you. I also believe that there are biblical standards in place for the proper order for publicly praying in tongues in order to be interpreted for prophecy. Please read 1 Corinthians 14:1-25 for further understanding.

Two powerful parts of supplication, stated in Philippians 4:6, are the thanksgiving and the peace of God. If life ever takes you to the place of supplication before your heavenly Father, then I believe you are at one of the highest forms of faith. Why, you might ask? Because you are presenting to the Lord a demand for a miracle, and when you come desperately, you are usually able to believe that he has the power to shift it and provide the answer needed. When you cry out to the Lord in deep sincerity, you must know that his heart can be so moved that he will push back death, reverse a ruling or judgment over your life, and release even more miracles that no one can explain. This is the power of supplication.

When I was in my twenties and trying to find my place in the world, one of my mentors, Attorney Sandra L. Jackson, gave me the most unique instructions for prayer. You never know what your mentor or coach may tell you to do, but if you believe they are called to train you, then you will submit and follow. I called her, needing direction because my request before God was major for that season in my life. This is what she said. *"Well, you need to pray. Go get these three things before you go to God: a glass of water, a blanket, and a box of tissues."* Ummmm, what? I was totally confused. Once again, she repeated the instructions and once again, I was perplexed. Hearing my complete lack of understanding over the phone, she explained further, *"Lay out the blanket, and keep the water and tissues close by. As you talk to the Lord, you will need to reach for them."* She was preparing me for supplication.

I had no clue, but I got my three things and sat on the blanket to pray. When I was done, I was laying flat on my stomach, tissues were all over the floor from wiping my tears, and the glass was empty. But wow oh wow; when I stood to my feet, I stood free, believing that the Lord had already come to my rescue. My spirit was empty of anxiety and full of hope. If you are in a desperate place, I suggest getting those three items, going to a private location and asking God for help? Don't worry about the details he'll work that out for you. Just stand up when your spirit is empty and your heart and mind are clear.

The second type of prayer is something I call **communing** with the Lord. I firmly believe that prayer is a conversation that doesn't always require you talking. Communing is sharing your intimate thoughts and feelings, especially when it is on a spiritual level. This is not an easy task. In fact, for many it may be easier to come to God with deep supplication. It requires focus and undivided attention. It means that the King wants to sit with me, and I acknowledge that his words are far more important than mine. Communing is relinquishing control over your self, over a matter...over all.

Since coaching is about asking questions for guidance, allow me to ask the following:

1. How far could you advance if you showed up to pray and didn't talk but just sat listening to God's instruction?

2. Are you overconfident in your ability to endlessly talk about yourself to the Creator when he is the one who already knows you through and through?

3. If you were forbidden to ask God to give you stuff, would you still show up to prayer?

It's good to know if it is pride and arrogance that drive us to our knees. Most avoid communing with God because they are afraid of what they'll find out about themselves or what the Lord will say to them. Some of us, who show up to commune with God, often journal our conversations. It's not a requirement or a measuring rod, but it's a great way of recording what God reveals to you when you linger with him. Sometimes the conversation is all written down to bring in your focus, and for review later when you've forgotten what your Lord spoke to you. Some record after they leave his presence. Still others hold the words deep in their hearts and trust that they could not possibly be forgotten. The "how" is not important. Communing is not legalistic. Communing is relational and exposes the intent of your heart to not just God but to you as well.

> Whenever Moses went out to the Tent of Meeting, all the people would get up and stand in the entrances of their own tents. They would all watch Moses until he disappeared inside. As he went into the tent, the pillar of cloud would come down and hover at its entrance while the LORD spoke with Moses.
> Inside the Tent of Meeting, the LORD would speak to Moses face to face, as one speaks to a friend.
> Afterward Moses would return to the camp, but the young man who assisted him, Joshua son of Nun, would remain behind in the Tent of Meeting.
> —EXODUS 33:8-9, 11 *New Living Translation*

I love reading through this account because of the movie I see playing in my mind. There's a descending of the Presence of God, there's conversation between God and man, there's man recognizing the power of God, and there's the intimacy of God's Presence. This is so powerful because Joshua (the next leader) would sit and watch this interaction. Perhaps that's why Joshua succeeded Moses, because he learned the art of leadership and communing. Never forget that when you leave a time of communing, then the glory of God, his Presence, goes with you wherever you go. You also receive his peace so that you don't return to life full of anxiety.

One of the effects of communing with God is worship. Worship is acknowledging who he is in all his majesty. Praise is thanking him for what he's done. When you commune with God, then worship drives you to remember his limitless power. Worship does not always require music, but it can. If you don't understand what songs are worship songs, look to the lyrics. Do the words guide you to a love affair? Do the lyrics tell of his power and strength as our King? That is worship. Inspirational, feel-good music has its place, but won't assist when you need to commune. Does it tug on your heart, and encourage an intimate encounter with the Lord? Then it's probably worship. If it speaks of what God does, then it would be praise. If it speaks of who God is, then it is worship. Remember, communing may feel awkward at first, as does dating someone new. But if you get out of the "me zone" and jump into the "God zone," then you may discover a new form of prayer that is full of wonder.

One of the last forms of prayer that you need to know in the coaching experience is **meditating.** I teach that meditating in prayer works best with the word of God. Affirmations are good, but are not to replace the word of God and our memorization or our confession of it. Mostly all of the children of our family memorize Psalm 1 and put their name in it as part of the their declaration. My daughter was reciting the passage at the age of three with great ease, because every night when she went to bed, we would meditate on it and repeat it. Here's an example of how you would meditate on Psalm 1:

> Blessed is Theresa
> Who walks not in the counsel of the ungodly,
> Nor stands in the path of sinners,
> Nor sits in the seat of the scornful;
> But Theresa's delight is in the law of the LORD,
> And in His law does she meditate day and night.
> Theresa shall be like a tree
> Planted by the rivers of water,
> That brings forth its fruit in her season,
> Theresa's leaf also shall not wither;
> And whatever Theresa does shall prosper.
>
> —PSALM 1:1-3 *New King James Version*

To meditate implies a mulling over and careful review. For example, sheep have four stomachs, so they eat grass and chew it over and over again. They eat, chew, swallow, regurgitate, chew again, swallow into the second stomach, regurgitate, chew again, swallow into the third stomach, regurgitate, chew again, and swallow into the fourth stomach. God wants us to chew on his word like sheep. To eat just one meal, will take sheep a day to process. We must do the same. Meditating can be praying a verse, from memory, through the reciting, and proclaiming of it. Meditating can also be reading it over and over. Studying it in various translations. Meditating can be talking to the Lord in prayer and telling him that you trust the promise of his word. Sometimes you rehearse a specific promise he made to you during your time of communing. Rehearsing it in prayer through meditating helps you to trust him more. When you are overwhelmed, you have to meditate, you must remember who God is.

> *I lie awake thinking of you,*
> *meditating on you through the night.*
> —PSALM 63:6 *New New Living Translation*

What you must remember is that there is power in prayer, and prayer is not legalistic but relational. Psalm 119 is the longest chapter in the Bible. It is a powerful tool to use for meditating on his **laws, precepts, statutes, commands, and ordinances.** In my discipleship program, Me Management, I suggest underlining when you see these five words to draw in your focus and meditation. This psalm is divided into sections of eight verses each under the different Hebrew alphabet. It is full of powerful scriptures that are perfect platforms for meditation.

In all my coaching, I would be misguided to tell you that you can find your mission without prayer. Honestly, you cannot survive without spending time with God. It's an investment. It's a sacrifice. It's a daily process. It's possible.

CHAPTER QUESTIONS

Is it difficult to come into God's presence knowing that you will be revealed? Explain.

Do you avoid intimate personal prayer and gravitate to corporate prayer? If yes, why?

Do you feel like formal religious words must be spoken and prayers uttered out loud to be heard?

COACHING VERSE (various translations)

[1 THESSALONIANS 5:17]
Pray continually.

[1 THESSALONIANS 5:17 *New King James Version*]
Pray without ceasing.

[1 THESSALONIANS 5:17 *New Living Translation*]
Never stop praying.

[1 THESSALONIANS 5:17 *Amplified Version*]
Be unceasing in prayer [praying perseveringly].

[1 THESSALONIANS 5:17 *The Message Bible*]
Pray all the time.

[1 THESSALONIANS 5:17 *New English Translation*]
Constantly pray.

DIVINE DECLARATION

Lord, I will find my "thing." Help me keep in touch with my inner little girl so that I will be pliable, submitted, and open to discovery.

CHAPTER 10
Types of mentoring

Yes, this is a book on coaching, but it is necessary to set you up for success with the second step on your spiritual development journey. In chapter 4 I noted the different types of spiritual growth platforms, and stated that mentoring was the stepping-stone after coaching. Because that is our next step, I want to point you in the right direction once you receive the necessary insight from this coaching relationship. There should always be a subsequent step in your development. Proper coaching opens your eyes to what needs to be done and how you can prepare for an overall life change. Here's an illustration to help you understand the breakdown of the YOU development. Think of it as the ultimate road trip!

THE YOU SPIRITUAL DEVELOPMENT JOURNEY:

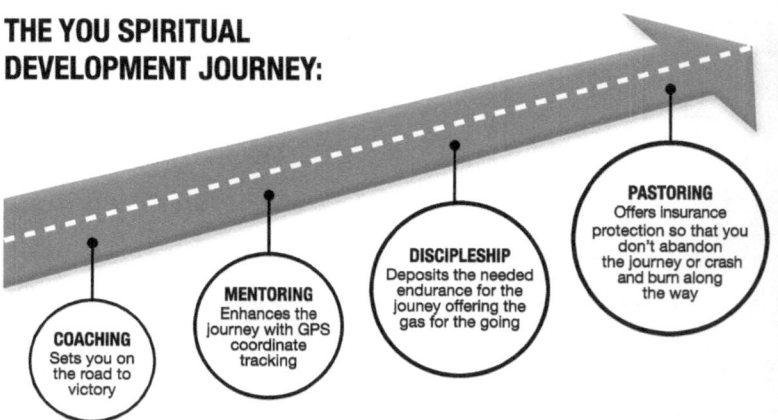

COACHING
Sets you on the road to victory

MENTORING
Enhances the journey with GPS coordinate tracking

DISCIPLESHIP
Deposits the needed endurance for the jouney offering the gas for the going

PASTORING
Offers insurance protection so that you don't abandon the journey or crash and burn along the way

Before we go into the types of mentoring, I want to reassure you that I don't claim to have all you need. Our relationship may fall into one of three categories. First, you may simply read this book, and I may just be a coach along your journey. Secondly, I may offer several tools that allow you to maximize your exposure to the ministry I offer, but you will grow with someone else as your pastor. And lastly, we may meet and build relationship and walk together through at least 3 of the steps on the YOU Spiritual Development Journey. Whatever the connection, I trust that you will seek godly counsel and leaders. There are many tremendous spiritual leaders in the kingdom of God, and none should compete for followers. Ultimately, I am a strong proponent that all Christians should experience coaching, mentoring, discipling and pastoring. Without these interactions, you may get stagnate and fail to bloom and fulfill your mission. Look at this verse that speaks of competition and comparison to different spiritual leaders. God is not a supporter of cliques.

> *For when one says, "I follow Paul,"*
> *and another, "I follow Apollos,"*
> *are you not mere human beings?*
> *What, after all, is Apollos? And what is Paul?*
> *Only servants, through whom you came to believe—*
> *as the Lord has assigned to each his task.*
> *I planted the seed, Apollos watered it,*
> *but God has been making it grow.*
> *So neither the one who plants nor the one who waters*

> is anything, but only God, who makes things grow.
> The one who plants and the one who waters
> have one purpose, and they will each be rewarded
> according to their own labor.
> For we are co-workers in God's service;
> you are God's field, God's building.
> By the grace God has given me, I laid a foundation
> as a wise builder, and someone else is building on it.
> But each one should build with care.
> For no one can lay any foundation other than
> the one already laid, which is Jesus Christ.
> —1 CORINTHIANS 3:9-11

Please be wise concerning your spiritual building process. No coach takes the place of your pastor. No mentor is all of what you need. There are several builders. If someone insists on being your mentor and claims to have everything you need, then you may want to run. I may coach you now and pastor you later. I may pastor you, and this should mean that I offer some form of discipleship as part of the journey. This discipling could come from someone else in the church, but it should be a program that will enhance the building being done as your pastor. Our goal at Hallel Chapel is to offer solid enhancements to the spiritual journey of those we shepherd. For example, we may use a book in Bible study written by someone not even connected to the church, to coach the church into powerful living.

Okay, are you ready to dig in? Let's roll up our sleeves and keep the lessons coming. Now, once you've been coached and recognize the need for step 2 in your development, then the mentoring process will more than likely include one or all of the following steps. The first type of mentoring is **inspiration**. There would be no need for mentoring if inspiration wasn't present. What is inspiration? You ask great questions!

> **in·spire** |inˈspī(ə)r| *verb* **1**: to fill someone with the urge to do or feel something.

Inspiration is the process of being stimulated. So a type of mentoring is found in the process of one being stimulated to take action in their life by another. This can take place through various avenues as the mentor displays parts of their life to others. This example brings about the "filling," which leads to the "stimulation" that takes you from where you are to where you want to be.

As with everything, there must be wisdom. So for each effect produced by mentoring, as your coach, I must also offer a warning. In this case, because of the stimulus associated with inspiration, you must be clear on how you control the attraction, which is the power of evoking interest or pleasure. A lot of times within us, life's brokenness mixes with a sudden burst of inspiration by someone, and we aren't fully sure what to do with this awakening. When you've been confused and are suddenly inspired and filled with the urge to do something, then you may just jump up and follow that person anywhere. Our society sometimes takes advantage of the act of inspiring, and at times, creates fanaticism, idolatry, or seduction. Therefore in your compulsion, please process where you are and what you need so that you can proceed with a correct focus. Do your homework on the person you want to follow. Make sure they live what they talk, and what they talk lines up with Christ.

One of the worse combinations in the world is a desperate mentee with an insecure mentor. That is a codependent disaster in the making. An insecure mentor finds worth in having a fan club, and as a result, they want to be idolized to feed their ego (Remember that goal?). Meanwhile, if the mentee is overly desperate, they will do anything to get approval. They may never be taught how to walk independently. Never maturing, they will be conditioned to lean on the mentor for everything. A proper coaching, mentoring, discipling, or pastoring model should include and enhance stability and encourage growth.

Another red flag for women to be aware of is what Evangelist Patricia Ashley calls "sexless lesbianism." As you are drawn to a mentor, keep tabs on the allurement. If codependency becomes a byproduct of this interaction, then the attraction can even become distorted in a sexual manner. I know this may sound ludicrous, but I want you to be wise. Some people think that if there is no physical interaction, you haven't crossed the line into sexual desire, please note that sexual attraction begins with an emotional connection. An adulterous affair, between a man and a woman, doesn't begin the minute a sexual encounter occurs but when the emotional bond is formed that leads to that encounter. All in all, I teach that God intends for us to have heterosexual relationships leading towards marriage, as this is his basis for procreation. When the mentoring connection between women enhances desires that lead inspiration into sexual attraction, I suggest that the relationship be severed. Focus and direction should be maintained. If the lines get blurred, then the journey becomes aimless. Your construction gets lost with the entrance of immorality.

The second type of mentoring characteristic is **imitation.** It is said that Imitation is the sincerest form of flattery. To imitate is to follow as a model.

im·i·ta·tion | ˌiməˈtāSH(ə)n| *noun* **1**: an observed behavior whereby an individual observes and replicates another's behavior

Before we dissect this characteristic, let's be clear that from a spiritual perspective, there is a specific chain of command for this process. I approach coaching and mentoring from a spiritual position, therefore, I would suggest that Christ is found in the midst of this process or you may open a door to imitating someone that distracts you from *conducting yourself* according to the word of God.

And you should imitate me, just as I imitate Christ.
—1 CORINTHIANS 11:1 *New Living Translation*

As phenomenal as Paul was in his impact on Christianity, he still maintained that if you imitate him, then he must imitate Christ. Proper order should never be overlooked. Imitating involves the process of noting something in your mentor and wanting to see that exhibited in yourself. It is a powerful form of transformation. It is the mentee understanding the processes the mentor followed (in their walk with the Lord) to become who they are. Imitation involves submitting to necessary change. You should expect that there would be instructions given to reach the change your desire. It is humbly stating that who you are is not all you can become. Mentoring should challenge you. It pushes you to the edge of the cliff, declaring that you jump off and learn to soar. Someone is examining you and instructing you to do more, if you want to be more. This is why mentoring is not a comfortable process, because imitation involves quite a bit of sacrifice. Never assume your mentor become who you admire without having to work hard, sacrifice and go through pain. You should see battle scars on a good mentor.

So if you want to imitate them, then you too will have to work hard, give up some things and go through pain.

In order to reach the desired results of imitation, we must be able to distinguish between submission and control. There will be a requirement for the mentee to submit, which is defined as yielding to a superior force or the authority. So many people misunderstand that word. However, submitting in order to grow requires your consent to go through a specific process. It doesn't have to be negative, as many assume, but it does require respect. I believe that if a mentee doesn't respect their mentor, then submission and growth will be impossible. How can you follow someone's guidance, suggestions, and wisdom if you don't believe they have much to offer?

Once I was attempting to mentor and disciple a young lady, but every time we met or I tried to make a deposit into her, I felt like I was hitting a brick wall. My prayer was that the Lord would reveal to me the root of the problem in order to make progress. One day, in a conversation with her and a couple other ladies, she blurted out to me, *"I don't want to be like you! Why would I want to be like you without a man, single, and not dating? That's not who I'm trying to be!"* Ahhh, there was the answer; she didn't respect where I was in my journey. I was living by the word's standards while I waited to be married. Well, I only replied that I didn't plan on being single for the rest of my life, but I was maximizing my time serving God while I was single. Nearly 15 years later I am married to an amazing man that loves me like no other could, with a precious daughter. The young woman and I are no longer connected. Unfortunately, not much of a transfer took place in that relationship due to a lack of respect.

Although, submission must be displayed, exhibited by the mentee, there is a mandate on the mentor as well. The mentor must not seek to control the person they are mentoring, but guiding them is the key. If a mentor places demands, rules, or limitations on your life that are not biblically sound, I'd be suspicious of where the training is leading. Or if they seek to intimidate you by force or fear, then that is not a healthy relationship, and once again leans toward codependency. In any mentoring relationship, the mentee should be free to go. At every level, the deposit can cease. If I'm coaching you through this book, you can always put it down. If I'm mentoring someone in the monthly Bloom sessions, they don't have to attend. Even in committing to the discipleship program, women have pulled out because they did not want to submit to the process. And lastly, church membership can always be withdrawn if you no longer want to be pastored by someone. There must always be an option to pull out of a relationship if you either refuse to do the required work or if you are being led into negative behavior. Now, a dedicated mentor may ask the mentee to press in and push until they breakthrough in life, but we should always have the right to exercise free will.

The difference between control and submission is that control seeks to restrict your free will and overpower your thinking creating inferiority and a lack of confidence. Submission, however, asserts that you are free to make your own choices, as you respect the deposit being made into you that is cultivating growth, maturity and communion with the Lord. Don't waste the time or anointing of the one who is there to help you bloom.

AN EXAMPLE OF SUBMISSION: a mentee is going home for the holidays and informs the mentor that they will be away for a two-weeks. They make plans to cover any work, duties, or training mutually agreed upon prior to leaving town. The mentor encourages the mentee to maintain the progress made while they are gone. They may even recommend that certain work be

in place for the mentor to follow during their trip. All is clear with both parties, and they either stay in loose contact during those two weeks, or they pick back up and meet upon the mentee's return.

AN EXAMPLE OF CONTROL: a mentee is going home for the holidays and informs the mentor that they will be away for a two-weeks. The mentor wants to know why this trip is even necessary. The mentor displays an angry temperament, demanding that the mentee explain why they did not ask for permission first. The mentor suggests that the mentee is a failure and heavily implies that the trip will doom their mentoring relationship, and that the mentee should no longer contact them upon their return.

Which seems like a healthier interaction, in your opinion? Always remember that even if you have to submit to a hard process, it should contribute to your growth. It may hurt, but advancement is on the other side. As long as Christ is part of the imitation process, both parties will be covered.

The last form of mentoring, and by no means the least, is found in **presentation.**

> **pre·sent** |prəˈzent| *verb* **1**: show or offer for others to scrutinize

Mentoring is akin to making an investment and collecting on your venture. Presentation is the result of inspiration and imitation. It's the end result, and others now take a look at the finished product. It is in essence a return on an investment. This may take months or years depending on the submission by the mentee and the investment of the mentor. I've mentored young girls and women for over twenty years, and honestly, not every deposit I've made has paid a dividend to them. There have been times when I've lost faith in the process and wondered if I was actually called into certain individual's lives. There have been times that the mentee just didn't want to break free from their dysfunction in order to invest in the building process. I can lead you to water, but only you can drink. I can give you piano lessons, but only you can spend time practicing. Honestly, mentors get tired. Quite frankly, sometimes we want more for the mentee than they want for themselves. But one thing I've learned over all these years is that if a person pulls on my gifts and really wants the relationship to work, that will inspire me to imitate Christ for them so they can be presented back to the Lord as a beautiful display of Christ's power as they learn to conduct themselves as a daughter of the King of Kings.

> *Work hard so you can present yourself to God and receive his approval. Be a good worker, one who does not need to be ashamed and who correctly explains the word of truth.*
> —2 TIMOTHY 2:15 (*New Living Translation*)

Sometimes a mentor can forget that they aren't building a replica of themselves. Mentees are not monuments to our greatness. We aren't presenting mentees to gain people's approval, but we're offering a presentation to the Lord. This causes me to tremble when I consider the weight of how you instruct a person in their development. God holds mentors accountable. If it is a spiritual platform, then there is a requirement that we answer to God and receive his approval. That is why spiritual mentoring cannot occur without a lot of prayer through supplication, communing, and meditating by both parties.

I'll be honest, I feel like Forest Gump. *"That's all I have to say about that."* It is now time for you to go out there and become the somebody you were created to be. I am not sure of the exact role I will play in your life, but if this is our only interaction in the world, my prayer is that we will connect in heaven. When God plays the Blu-ray disk of your life, it will show that you were cultivated to bloom into a glorious creature of praise for his glory. **Be the YOU the Creator intended.**

CHAPTER QUESTIONS

Have you ever been inspired by someone's life and took steps to connect with them? If so, explain.

Have you ever been stifled by someone's attempted control over your life? Explain.

Have you ever grown as a result of submitting to a great leader? Or do you think you can grow as a result of submitting to a spiritual leader? Explain.

COACHING VERSE

[2 TIMOTHY 1:5-7 *The Message Bible*]
That precious memory triggers another: your honest faith—and what a rich faith it is, handed down from your grandmother Lois to your mother Eunice, and now to you! And the special gift of ministry you received when I laid hands on you and prayed—keep that ablaze! God doesn't want us to be shy with his gifts, but bold and loving and sensible.

DIVINE DECLARATION

When someone is willing to deposit truth into my life, I will cherish it and nourish my growth. I look to be inspired, so that I may imitate, in order to be presented to the Lord as the creature he intended me to be.

PART THREE

RESOURCES

⁓ MEETING YOUR NEEDS ⁓
A Coaching Assessment Questionnaire
Theresa McFaddin Ordell © 2015

1] Are you a Christian? If so, for how long? If not, are you encouraged to believe in Jesus Christ as a result of this book? Explain.

2] If you are a Christian, does your lifestyle exhibit fruit from your faith in Christ and convictions as a believer?

3] Do the women closest to you inspire you to live in a godly manner? How do they encourage your faith?

Meeting Your Needs | 131

4] Do you currently study the Word of God on a consistent basis? Is this based on a study guide, program or a random reading of scripture? Explain.

5] How often do you attend church?

6] Are you currently being pastored, if you attend church does the pastoral staff or pastor know who you are and offer assistance with your needs through the various church ministry groups and classes?

7] Have you ever been coached or mentored? Please elaborate if so.

8] Who in your life challenges you and requires you to be accountable?

9] Based on the teaching in this book, is there a balance between the girl you were and the woman you are?

10] Do you know your life mission? If so, what steps have you taken to further this call?

11] Which option best explains where you are on your life mission and why: a) searching for a mission; b) working it, but needing encouragement; c) hit a wall and about to quit; in need of a life line.

12] What actions has this book sparked (encouraged, inspired, emboldened you to take)?

ASSESSMENT DIRECTION

- If you had difficulty answering questions 1-6, your needs fall under the **discipleship and pastoring** stages for spiritual growth. I would strongly recommend finding a Bible believing church that teaches the Word of God. In addition, you should become part of a discipleship program to build your Christian faith. Me Management is a 10-month women's discipleship program that I've created that teaches how the Bible influences you in critical areas of life. You will find more information under resources. We do offer online options.

- If you had difficulty answering questions 7-12, your needs fall under the **coaching and mentoring** stages for spiritual growth. I recommend finding a mentor to guide you in your quest to develop, define and execute your life mission. We offer monthly Bloom sessions in the Los Angeles area. Also, you can go to our resource page for further online options. Various events can be accessed online if you continue to check our website for details.

- If you had a general struggle with answering 5 or more of these questions, feel free to review our available resources to point you toward growth. You may also send an email for further assistance in your quest.

～ COACHING **YOU** ～
Questionnaire
Supplement for book © by T. McFaddin Ordell

The purpose of this Questionnaire is to help you examine a lot of your specific life activity so as to evaluate your behavior and discover your needs based upon the YOU Spiritual Development Journey.

1] List 3 of your short-term goals.

2] List 3 of your long-term goals.

3] Do you own property or have plans to do so within the next couple of years?

4] Do you invest in any stocks, mutual funds or saving plans?

5] Do you work on a nonspecific job or are you working in a chosen career position?

6] Are you making a comfortable salary or on the set path to make that money in the future?

7] Outside of your job or career, what other fields of study or programs have you participated in?

8] What are your most advantageous skills or gifts?

9] Are you in school to further your education?

10] What level of education or certification have you completed?

11] Are you involved in community service?

12] Are you a member of a word teaching church, and if so what are your ministry duties?

13] During the course of a week, how much time is given to social activities?

14] Do you keep and use an appointment book to maintain daily, weekly and monthly activities?

15] What are your hobbies or social activities outside of work?

16] During the course of a week how many times do you cook?

17] How many hours of sleep do you require a night to be functional or to feel rested the following day?

18] Do you set one particular day of the week to clean your house or do you consistently clean your house throughout the week?

19] How many times a week do you have personal devotion?

20] Do you exercise regularly at a gym, park or through some type of sport activity?

21] How often do you get your hair and nails done and do you invest in any other beauty treats?

22] When's the last time you've been to the doctor or dentist for a check up of some sort?

23] Of your 3 closest friends, how do you define their strong points and weak points?

24] Do you mentor children in a formal or informal way?

25] If you are married, what have been the most influential enhancements to your life by your mate?

26] Do you have difficulty expressing your feelings in your marriage or dating relationship?

27] Is your prayer time for your marriage or dating relationship based upon your request for your own better treatment or your mate's personal development and blessings?

28] If you are single, are you still on speaking terms with the men you are no longer dating seriously?

29] If you are single, is it hard for you to meet men that are able to live up to your expectations?

30] If you are single, do you find a lack of men in your life that are just really good friends?

31] If you are single, do you constantly deal with issues of loneliness?

32] If you have children, what programs are they active in and which do you volunteer for?

33] If you have children, what are the names of their closest friends and parents?

34] If you have children, do any of the school administrators know you as a concerned parent?

35] If you have children, what are each child's gifts and talents?

36] If you are a single parent, how many men have you dated in the last year and how do they interact with your child or children?

37] If you are a single parent, do you have rules about men spending the night with you?

38] If you are a single parent, are the men you date ever alone with your child and how many dates do you go on before they are allowed to even meet your children?

39] From your past broken friendships, have you initiated forgiveness and reconciliation?

40] From your past broken friendships, have you been open to those that come back wanting peace and offering apologies?

41] Do you have any unresolved problems with family members?

42] Do you find it hard to forgive someone who has hurt you or are you open to discussing the situation with the one that you have problems with?

43] Do you presently or in your past have problems with drug or alcohol use?

44] Are you easily agitated when things don't go your way?

45] Are you a newly saved Christian or how long have you been walking in a committed Christian life?

46] Do you find it difficult to blend your beliefs as a Christian with your daily lifestyle?

47] Do you actively work on building and establishing your relationship with Jesus Christ?

48] What areas of your life can you directly show changes that are a result of your prayer life?

49] Do you find that you give up on yourself after too many let downs?

50] If you were to rate your overall life development on a scale of 1 to 10 (10 being the most stable rating), what would it be?

DIVINE DECLARATIONS
Theresa McFaddin Ordell © 2015

Lord, I will find my "thing." Help me keep in touch with my inner little girl so that I will be pliable, submitted, and open to discovery.

I, the creature will praise you, the Creator, because I'm pretty wonder-full! Lord, I want to know who I am full well, free of doubt, and accepting of what you decide to change.

God of the Angel Armies comes to my rescue with unlimited resources of hope, peace, and love. He's the Almighty! I have been transplanted into the Lord's own garden!

God I will allow you to use my mentor to fashion me to be the best I can be, by teaching me through their victories and challenges. I will respect the process.

If my success depends on how other people treat me, I will never become anything. But if I become a success in spite of this, then I have achieved a great victory. I will succeed! God is more than the world against me!

Dear Lord, I want to be a woman that listens and worships you. I want to know when to push forward and when to lean on you. Balance me and make me over. May the God of Peace send the Prince of Peace to give me perfect Peace.

Dear Lord, I want YOU. Dear Lord, I need YOU. Help me decrease so you can increase in me.

Lord, although I desire things ultimately, I am driven to possess inward sufficiency through godly living. Bless me according to your unlimited resources deposited in my inner woman.

Lord, draw me closer to you in prayer as the deer pants for water. Send me out with your Presence and help me find peace regardless of my circumstances.

When someone is willing to deposit truth into my life, I will cherish it and nourish my growth. I look to be inspired, so that I may imitate, in order to be presented to the Lord as the creature he intended me to be.

MY TOP 10 SHARED SOCIAL MEDIA NUGGETS

Theresa McFaddin Ordell © 2015

Want to know what to expect if you follow me on Facebook or Twitter? Here are 10 post I've shared in the last year that people "liked".

1] My father was an entrepreneur.

My mother is an entrepreneur.

My husband is an entrepreneur.

I am an entrepreneur.

These are some of the things I've learned first hand:

You have to take risks.

You have to expect some margin of failure.

You have to put in some hard work.

You have to shut out those with limited vision.

You have to push through darkness and demand to see the light.

You have to be coached, mentored and sponsored in some way.

My dad had John DeLorean. My mom had Dr. Juanita Smith and more. My husband has Bishop Thompson and more. I have my mom and more.

Get a plan.

Follow through.

Go with your gut.

Get up when you fall.

Release your internal potential.

and Pray without ceasing because you can only make it if God steps in and works some miracles on your behalf! (break over—now back to my work cave) #coachingYOU #pastorT# #getonamission #girlonamission #stayonamission

2] Some people make excuses & there are moments when some people have a valid emergency. You can only know the difference when you are 1 or all of the following:
1) objective
2) discerning
3) full of grace
4) someone who has needed another to be 1-3 before

3] Cultural Holiness causes us to drift from our Faith. The Bible must be our measuring rod for actions not our feelings or friends. #pastorT

4] Singles—I know you are a master of menu ordering & can name most of the hot eating spots on your Yelp territory...but ummmm...you need to start prepping for that marriage you're praying for! Practice and serve people at work. Practice cooking and serve men that are your brothers. Practice and serve the marrieds at your church (as you should go to church). Swap recipes with your single girlfriends so you all can make brothers call their grandmothers and brag! #getonamission

5] Wives—please cook something! Even if you aren't working with chef skills log on to allrecipe.com and make that house a home! My mother used to say one of the sexiest scents in your home should be something good cooking in the kitchen!

I'm a little overwhelmed right now with deadlines—this thing—that thing—the other thing... BUT Saturday I made red beans with smoked turkey, and today I made baked fish with seafood dressing and greens. Make enough to stretch over the days if you can't cook daily, but show those men some love in all areas! #thatsall #girlonamission

6] Marrieds:

Pray together—that's your power base! When you stand before God as a team your union is strengthened. Pray about communication, wise money habits, purpose in ministry, sexual satisfaction, favor in business, witty inventions and blessed health. Pray for your extended families! Pray against sexual immorality entering your relationship! Pray daily! Don't miss moments to shift your atmosphere!

7] Marrieds:

If you pray TOGETHER for sexual satisfaction IN MARRIAGE—that means from each other! And you have to be willing to have sex with each other to make it happen. And you have to communicate about what satisfaction means. (Yep, this post actually has the words "sex" & "marriage" in the same sentence—who knew)

Singles:
This is not for you to practice without a license. ... you'd be surprised how the satisfaction & marriage part will not be that easy if you go out of order. You get a license for your pet, to drive, to work... why not to secure sex? Ok, good night! #justsaying

8] TODAY:

Reconnect with your God.
Reconnect with your calling.
Reconnect with your life.
You cannot surrender. Endure.
#soulhunger #findyoursoul

9] YOU—YES YOU!
YOU are victorious!
YOU are overcoming!
YOU are redeemed!
YOU are worth the Blood He shed!
YOU HAVE A FUTURE IN GOD!
#weshine #weconquer #ohtheblood

10] The power behind Prophetic Worship—is that you are trained to flow with God in the unknown. You are trained to follow God in an uncomfortable place. You have to abandon the songs that worked in the past and look for a heavenly sound that sings to your future! You have to listen—You have to want it—You have to need a fresh revelation!!! If you want the old, then don't look for a prophetic move. If you don't want the prophetic power, then do you really want to worship?
#strangechurch #weshine #GROW

ᜃ WHERE TO GO FROM HERE ᜄ

- A Date with God Annual Getaway
- No Room For Excuses book
- www.adatewithGod.com
- Audio links

- #GIRLSONAMISSION
- Monthly Bloom Sessions
- www.girlsonamission.us

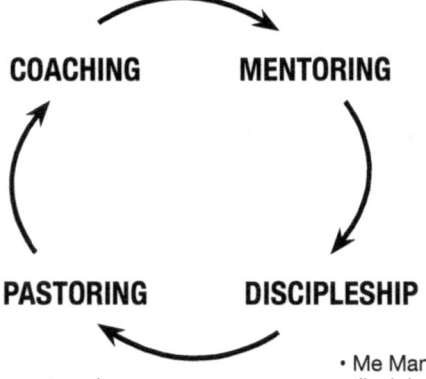

COACHING **MENTORING**

PASTORING **DISCIPLESHIP**

- Hallel Chapel
- Church services, outreach
- Ongoing ministry
- Audio links and books
- www.hallelchapel.org

- Me Management weekly discipleship programs
- www.memanagement.org

Email: info@girlsonamission.us
Book website: www.coachingyoubook.com
Booking: use our speakers request form on the coaching website
Me Management Discipleship:
www.facebook.com/therealmemanagement
#girlsonamission website: www.girlsonamission.us
Church website: www.hallelchapel.org
Church app: TeamHallel - available for Android & iPhone
Twitter: www.twitter.com/harvestwords
Facebook: www.fb.com/datewithGod
Facebook: www.fb.com/teamhallel

Online class and session options are
available for your virtual connection.

#girlsgear: order your #GIRLSONAMISSION T-shirt on our websites

Social Media tags:
#coachingYOU
#girlsonamission
#pastorT
#bloomtime
#adatewithGod
#findyoursoul

 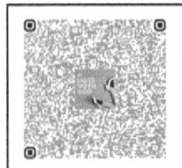 

www.ingramcontent.com/pod-product-compliance
Lightning Source LLC
Chambersburg PA
CBHW030444300426
44112CB00009B/1153